Happy 50th ... 14.?.96.

to bring b...

of the Af...

your life!!!

All love always.

Pat & Don

xx xx

CW01667697

AN AFRICAN SKETCHBOOK

Nandi woman

AN AFRICAN SKETCHBOOK

Drawings & Watercolours of Kenya by Ray Nestor with extracts from his memoirs

FOUNTAIN PRESS

To my wife, Dorothy

Fountain Press Limited
45 The Broadway
Tolworth
Surrey KT6 7DW
England

ISBN 0 86343 185 2

© Fountain Press Limited 1988

© Illustrations Ray Nestor 1988

All rights reserved
No part of this book may be
reproduced in any form
or by any means without
the permission of Fountain Press Ltd.

Extract from 'Out of Africa'
courtesy of the Estate
of Karen Blixen,
Putnam & Co, Publishers,
Random House, Inc.

Design and Layout by Grant Bradford

Typeset in Cheltenham Old Style
by Crowborough Typesetters

Printed and Bound by Amadeus, Italy

CONTENTS

Foreword 6

Introduction 8

British Rule 8

The Colonial Services 9

The Journey to Kenya 12

Mombasa to Nairobi 14

Hunting and Safaris 16

Nairobi in 1912 20

The Survey Department 24

The 1914–18 War

England 1915 26

Joining-up 27

France 27

The First Battle of the Somme 28

Back to England 30

Kenya after the Armistice 32

The Indian Question 32

The Harry Thuku Riot 33

The Soldier Settlement Scheme 34

Safari to Ithangu 36

My A-farm 40

Nairobi Life 43

The Muthaiga Club 44

Kenyan Characters 44

Jim Corbett 46

Lord Delamere 48

Lt. Colonel Ewart Scott Grogan 48

Denys Finch-Hatton 49

Lake Naivasha 50

The 'Boom' of the 1920s 53

The Building Scheme 54

The Slump 56

Life at Kipkarren 60

The Grass Fire Ordinance 68

World War II 72

Overland to Mombasa 73

Mombasa 74

Nyali 76

Malindi 77

Gedi 78

Moiben 80

Return to Kipkarren 81

The Nandi Native Tribe 84

Initiation Ceremonies 88

Nandi Costume 89

Building our House and Life on the Farm 92

Italian POWs 93

Dairy Farming 96

Nandi Customs 97

The Dam 100

Sale of the Farm 104

The Mountains of the Moon 106

Last Days at the Farm 108

Acknowledgments 111

Nandi Woman

Foreword

Africa has sanctuaries where creatures in danger of extinction take shelter in an ever more hostile and contracting environment. In the unlikely purlieus of Muthaiga Club outside Nairobi is to be found just such a sanctuary, maintained for the protection not of an endangered species but of an endangered custom: the seclusion of the British male. In the Members' Room no female foot may tread. But mine has, escorted by a very senior member. At a time when the East African male, like the lions he formerly hunted, may be expected to be enjoying a siesta, I tiptoed reverently in to inspect a picture hanging on a wall. That picture is undoubtedly the best known of the many drawings made in Kenya by Ray Nestor over a period of nearly fifty years. It is a sketch of an early settler, Berkeley Cole, Lord Delamere's brother-in-law, who started a fashion for draping a brightly coloured Somali shawl over his shoulders.

Ray Nestor's modesty as a painter has stood between him and a wider recognition of his work. He has never courted publicity, being content to record his impressions of a fascinating country and its diverse peoples for his own satisfaction and that of his friends. He arrived in the East Africa Protectorate, as Kenya then was, in 1912, only seventeen years after the British flag had been run up over the Commissioner's residence in Mombasa. Although the Uganda Railway had already opened up the country to the influence and commerce of the outside world the fundamental changes to come were, so to speak, only nibbling at the edges. Ray Nestor and his generation saw the country and its peoples very much as they had been for centuries; later, after the First World War when he fought in France and was severely wounded, he was to see those changes come about. His work as a surveyor took him to all parts of the country. Retiring from government service in the 1930s he and his wife turned to farming in an especially beautiful region, the Nandi hills in western Kenya, where they survived drought, locusts and the great depression, followed by the exigencies of the Second World War, until they retired in 1950 and finally came to rest in Sussex.

In all his time in Africa Ray Nestor was seldom without his paints and sketchbook, alert to capture the fugitive moment: an old Nandi woman in her beads and bangles drawing on her long pipe; a dhow in full sail beyond the coral reef outside Mombasa harbour; the stupendous view from his farm-house over down and forest rolling away towards Mount Elgon; a pair of rhinos threading their way through the bush under the snows of Kilimanjaro. These paintings are what they claim to be, sketches, with all the freshness, spontaneity and transcience of the sketch as against the set piece. The dragon-fly of art, as against the studied landscape over which it hovers.

When Ray Nestor was born in India in 1888 Queen Victoria had thirteen years yet to reign and the British Empire was at the zenith of its confidence and strength. The publication of this selection from his many sketches has been timed to concide with his one hundredth birthday. I am sure that everyone who turns its pages will warmly congratulate him on no mean achievement in preserving on paper visions of fleeting moments that can never come again.

Elspeth Huxley
May 1988

Nandi Elmoran

Introduction

The explorations of Livingstone and Stanley in darkest Africa which many of us read about in our childhood, appears to have taken place in very remote times, and yet both of these explorers died within the last hundred years, Stanley as recently as 1904. That was only eight years before my first arrival in Kenya in November 1912, or the British East Africa Protectorate as it was then called.

Looking back on those early days, I am thankful that I had the privilege of knowing this beautiful country before the end of an era. Until the First World War it was, as it had been for hundreds, perhaps for thousands of years, a primitive and virgin land. The animals lived, thrived and multiplied in their millions without much interference from man. The native population also lived, as they had done for centuries, in their huts, dressed in leather garments obtained from animals they had killed with bows and arrows or with their spears. Their bodies were decked out with bead ornaments or coiled wire, and their heads were plastered with ochre. They raided each other and stole the women and cattle from their neighbours. It was the accepted way of life and doubtless provided just that necessary touch of variety to their otherwise drab and uneventful existences.

And then the white man arrived with his new ideas and marvellous inventions. It was not a sudden invasion; rather a gradual infiltration, accelerated by outside influences, chiefly exploration and trade. But it is not to be assumed that it was a one-sided bargain, contact with Europeans conferred many benefits on the native population. Peace and prosperity reigned where, before the arrival of the British, any individual who strayed beyond the boundaries of his tribal influence was likely to be attacked and killed.

Not only this, but the natives now received expert medical attention. The death rate from infant mortality decreased to an astonishing extent, as did that from many prevalent diseases. One outstanding and very noticeable complaint was that of Yaws. At one time, the sufferers from this disgusting and contagious skin complaint of suppurating sores, were to be seen in large numbers in the streets of Nairobi. But the treatment, which I was informed consisted chiefly of injections of bismuth, appeared to work miraculously, until within a few years Yaws had been completely eradicated.

British Rule

The history of British rule in Kenya may be considered to have started in 1877 when the Sultan of Zanzibar, who was impressed with the advantages likely to result from closer association with British commercial interests, offered Sir William MacKinnon of the British East African Association, the concession of Customs and Administration along the east coast of Africa.

This coastal area was extended to a depth of 200 miles by making treaties with the African tribes of the interior. In 1888, the year of my birth, it became a Chartered Company of the British Government, with the title of the Imperial British East African Company.

At the same time, the British Government agreed to build the railway from the coast at Mombasa to Kisumu on Lake Victoria, a distance of 587 miles. This railway was called the Uganda Railway, although at that time, and for many years, it did not touch the soil of Uganda.

The object of the Uganda Railway was to open up the country, and to stop the iniquitous Arabic slave trade reported by Livingstone, who exposed the suffering of the slaves in the English newspapers. He was of the opinion that due to the dreadful conditions, not one-tenth of the numbers that started on their journey to the coast reached their destination. Early explorers describe the massacres of thousands of people who were speared to death in tribal raids.

As a result of these exposures, the people of England agreed to the expenditure necessary for the building of the railway.

While I was still in Kenya, a native who had been a slave and had been intimately connected with Livingstone was living in the country, he was called Mathew Wellington but his real name was Chengwinbi. In 1935 he died in Mombasa at the age of 90. Wellington was one of those who carried the body of his master from Lake Bangweulu, in Northern Rhodesia as it was then called, to the coast in 1873. As a child he was sold into slavery, but was rescued by a British cruiser and taken to Bombay where he came into contact with the Church Missionary Society, and in this way got to know Dr Livingstone.

When Livingstone was considered to have been lost after a long interval without any news of him, Stanley was commissioned by the *New York Herald* to go to Africa to search for him and they met at Ujije, where he greeted the explorer with the historic remark, 'Dr Livingstone, I presume?'

Later, when Livingstone was very ill with dysentry, his natives carried him on an improvised stretcher through the swamps to Chitambo village, where he died. His servants then roughly embalmed his body, enclosed it in a cylinder of bark, lashed the body to a pole and carried it from there to Bagamoyo, a distance of 1,500 miles. This is a remarkable example of loyalty and affection between the natives of the country and their white masters, and certainly most of us early settlers could testify to feelings of real friendship with our own servants, in pre-war days.

The newspaper, the *East African Standard* was instrumental in persuading the Government of Kenya to award a pension to this grand old man, Mathew Wellington.

Those of us who were in Kenya before the First World War may be considered to have been a link with this period of darkest Africa, and to have experienced much the same conditions known to the great explorers, not only Livingstone and Stanley, but Murchison, Lugard and Speke.

The Colonial Services

In 1912 I had my living to earn, and that was a problem at a time when unemployment was as high as it has ever been. And yet England was at the peak of her power and wealth. I seem to remember that the National Debt was under £100m. It is curious that when labour is very cheap the country is at its most prosperous stage.

I searched the advertisement columns of the newspapers and applied for every post I saw, including such appointments as that of Chief Engineer of the Uganda

Railway, for which I was, of course, quite unqualified with no experience. However, it turned out to be a move to my advantage, as I cannot otherwise account for the unexpected but very welcome offer, at a later date, of a job in the Survey Department in Kenya. It was lucky for me, and for many other young men, that the Crown was expanding and recruiting for the various departments of the Colonial Services.

A letter arrived from the Crown Agents for the Colonies instructing me to present myself for an interview at their offices in Whitehall Gardens. Appointments to the Colonial Services were made by selection, not by examination.

I was interviewed by a young man who confirmed that the job in the Survey Department was available, and he also offered me a much better job in the Colonial Audit. This I foolishly refused, as I considered my education as an engineer would be wasted. The opportunities for advancement and pay in the Audit were very good, and I often wondered, as the years went by, how varied my life would have been if I had made a different choice.

The first thing I did was to get an advance of one month's salary. Waiting in the banking department of the Crown Agents was a senior official of the Colonial Service in Kenya, who was very angry with the bank teller for the delay in dealing with his affairs. He complained that he had important matters to attend to, and that he administered a territory half the size of England. The teller at the counter gave me a sly wink.

At this time very little was known about the East African Protectorate or Nairobi, many people confused it with the territories on the West Coast, and even with South Africa. The officials at the Crown Agents and the Colonial Office were little better informed.

As a help to prepare ourselves for what we were to expect, recruits to the service received the East African Protectorate Handbook, which gave advice and warnings to new arrivals. We were told what to wear and what to take with us by way of equipment. The rays of the tropical sun were considered to be particularly dangerous, and we should never venture out in it, even for short distances, without a pith helmet, and preferably a spine pad as well.

Notes for officers appointed to East Africa and Uganda stated:

'Office hours in Nairobi are 9–4.'

'On the whole of these uplands the climate is excellent and invigorating.'

'The price of goods is higher than at home, the rupee (valued at one shilling and four pence) very nearly taking the place of the shilling.'

'His outfit should include thin clothing for the Red Sea, a sun hat, an umbrella (for going ashore at Port Said, Aden, Djibouti and Mombasa) and deck shoes.'

'The heat of the Red Sea is sometimes very oppressive and the continuous perspiration renders the system very thirsty. There is no harm in drinking large quantities of liquids, only alcohol should be taken very sparingly and the stronger forms of spirits eschewed altogether.'

'There is a pernicious system in the country of signing a chit for an article instead of paying for it; of this the newcomer should beware, as it lends itself to overestimating one's income.'

A portrait of Ray Nestor by Voll drawn at Port Said in the early 1920's

'The first lesson to be learnt is that great care must be taken in the regular use of the mosquito curtain (a heavy type).' There were also notes under such headings as: 'Precautions against malaria, sleeping sickness, tick fever, dysentery, jiggers, worms, plague.'

Also included was a chapter on the 'Treatment of Diseases and Accidents', this referred particularly to malaria, prickly heat and bites of poisonous snakes although it was added, 'they say snake bites are rare . . . do not walk the patient about, and do not give unlimited alcohol as both tend to promote the circulation and hasten the absorption of the injected poison.'

Broken limbs and lion bites (no mention of these being rare!) 'thoroughly swab out each hole and laceration with pure carbolic oil.'

Finally there was a page on Civil Uniforms for higher officials described as follows, '1st and 2nd class: 3 buttons; 3rd and 4th class 2; 5th class, 1 button.' I never discovered to which class I belonged and there was never an occasion for me to appear in any uniform, presumably this applied to Governors and senior officials if and when they attended a levée or perhaps to be awarded some decoration at Buckingham Palace.

The prospect of leaving dear old London, and of having to face the discomforts and possible dangers of a primitive country, made no appeal to me. So it was with dismay and misgiving that I made my preparations to go to Kenya.

The Journey to Kenya

Officials appointed to posts in the Colonies and Protectorates, such as Kenya and Uganda, were given their passages by sea, usually by steamers of the Union Castle or the P. & O. Line, through the Suez Canal and down the East Coast of Africa.

And so, in November 1912, I got a berth on the *Guelph* en route for Mombasa. It was a small steamer of about 4,500 tons, and its chief claim to fame was that it had been the last vessel to sight the ill-fated *Waratar* before it sank near Durban without trace. That disaster has remained one of the greatest mysteries of the sea, not only on account of there being no survivors, but also because no lifeboats or other wreckage identified with it, were ever washed up on the shores of South Africa.

The passenger lists of the *Guelph* contained the names of many well known Kenya officials and settlers, among the latter was that of Gibbs of Nakuru, as he was called, since he was the first to build a hotel and open shops in the town which has since grown to be among the biggest in Kenya.

Travel in those little steamers in which there were few passengers, probably not more than three score, was far more enjoyable than that on the larger vessels. Small as it was, it sported an orchestra consisting of the stewards and we danced to their music, in spite of the prodigious movement of the deck due to the heavy seas – very much more noticeable in these little boats. The whole party would sway from one end of the deck to the other as the boat rolled from side to side, but it somehow provided an extra zest to the fun, as we clung to each other for support.

By the end of the three weeks' voyage, the ship's passengers had developed into a happy family, making friendships which lasted a lifetime. The sights and experiences were all very new to us. Port Said was our first sight of the East. We were told that Port Said could be dangerous for strangers and we were advised to remain in large parties. Here the Simon Artz shop was the centre of attraction, and the women bought amber necklaces and beautifully embroidered shawls for ridiculous prices. Handfuls of moonstones were offered to us for the price of a few shillings, and most of us had our caricature portraits painted in crayons by Voll, whose work, as it accumulated, became world famous.

The *Guelph* arrived in Mombasa at the end of November 1912. There were no quays or wharfs for her to berth and unload in the old harbour, so we anchored out at sea and were taken ashore with our luggage in rowboats.

I had read about the coral island of Mombasa, and vaguely expected to see some evidence of the pretty pink coral of which young ladies' necklaces are made, but was disappointed. Nor was there any resemblance to the imaginative and illusive 'Better Land' so charmingly described by Mrs Hemans, which had appealed so much to me as a child.

> Where the burning rays of the ruby shine
> And the diamond lights up the secret mine,
> And the pearl gleams forth from the coral strand.

On the other hand, there was very much to see and to wonder at in this brief look around; first among these was the fantastic baobab tree, whose trunk is 20 or 30 feet thick, and which gives the impression of a massive uprooted tree planted upside-down with its roots in the air.

Our first duty was to find some accommodation, of which there was very little available, but we were allowed to doss down in a spare room in Mombasa Club for the night, till we reported our arrival to the authorities and were given our tickets for the train to Nairobi.

Mombasa to Nairobi

That first journey from Mombasa to Nairobi was a revelation. Never again shall I, or anyone else, have the opportunity of seeing so vast an accumulation of game. The herds extended on both sides of the railway line in their tens of thousands, as far as the eye could see; here were intermixed zebra, antelope and giraffe, which ran alongside and at times blocked the line to such an extent that the train was brought to a standstill. The animals were so tame and unafraid they stood about and had to be driven away with sticks before we could proceed.

It is curious that wild animals appear to accept a mechanical contrivance such as a train or car as being harmless, whereas the sight of a man will usually drive them into a panic. An exception is the rhino, who is a stupid creature and liable to charge on sight; one of them was known to have tried this with a railway engine causing considerable damage – no doubt to both parties!

During our journey up to Nairobi we were thrilled to see a mother giraffe defending her calf, she stood over her young one with legs apart, lashing out as two lions circled around her. She looked very ungainly and the calf appeared to be in danger of being crushed by her. It was such a sight that the train slowed down and two of the passengers tried to stop it while they got off to shoot the lions; this was not considered to be a very unreasonable request. The procedure was so casual and passengers had even been known to take over the job of driving the train.

The railway carriages were of quite a different pattern to the modern type. They consisted of a double compartment divided by a partition with four berths and a verandah at each end.

It was from a carriage of this type that one of the most amazing tragedies occurred, as described by Patterson, in his book *The Maneaters of Tsarvo.* Four men were asleep in the carriage as it travelled through the night, when the sliding door of the verandah opened and a lion entered. It grasped one of the men in its teeth and jumped out before the others could come to his help. This event took place only a few years before my arrival, and I met one of the occupants of the carriage, a foreigner. A curious feature of this adventure, if I remember rightly, was that the lion straddled the occupant of the lower berth but took the man on the top bunk and then jumped out of the window.

The rickety old Uganda train chugged its way over unevenly-laid sleepers, disturbing clouds of red dust which infiltrated into everything. The seats were covered with it as were our clothes and faces.

At some of the larger stations, such as Voi, we hurried out to have our lunch or dinner in one of the station's waiting-rooms. There were no facilities for meals on the train. The station itself was practically the only building at Voi except for a few *dukas* or shops in small corrugated iron buildings. At one of these shops we bought a tin of biscuits, which turned out to be such old stock, it was quite uneatable. The Indians who ran these shops must be given the credit of being the most enterprising pioneer traders in the country. You would find an Indian shop in some of the loneliest parts – even in the heart of a native reserve.

On our arrival at Nairobi Station, I, together with some other Government officials on first appointment, were met by the transport officer of the name of Noon. He was one of the best-known personalities in Kenya, and many a new

Boats viewed from deck of steamer at Port Said, with their gaily coloured produce for sale to passengers

arrival feeling lost and unhappy in an unfamiliar country was grateful to him for his friendly greeting, advice and help. He arranged for our luggage to be sent to the hotel at which we intended to stop, and advised us what amount the ricksha 'boys' should be paid.

I had intended to stop at the cheaper Stanley Hotel, then situated in Government Road, leading away from the station, but the ricksha boys decided to take me on to the Norfolk Hotel, half-a-mile or more further along. We passed the Stanley, a double-storey wooden building with a corrugated iron roof. It was so unimpressive, it never occurred to me that it was one of the two main hotels of Nairobi.

The Norfolk was considered to be the better hotel of the two, but the wood and iron structure was almost equally dreary, consisting as it did of a dining room, sitting room, bar and verandah in front, with the bedrooms at the back.

Hunting and Safaris

Life in the hotel, however, was by no means dull. It had an international reputation with big game hunters and American millionaires. They arrived in large parties accompanied frequently by their womenfolk decked out in the latest fashions. At dinner time they were very resplendent in evening dress and flashing jewels.

There was a continuous stream of important people, among them the American President Teddy Roosevelt, and the Duke of Sutherland, then Lord Stafford. The latter I remember particularly, as his valet, when they were leaving, sold large quantities of camp equipment and clothes; they were in perfect condition and of far better quality than we could buy in the town. I recall that I wore a couple of pairs of pyjamas for years, adorned with a ducal crown.

The hunting 'safaris' started from the hotel under the control of the big game hunters who organised and accompanied them.

The loads, which were made up to be approximately 60 pounds, were carried by the native porters; as many as a hundred or more. A large proporation of the loads were 60-pound bags of mealie-meal or ground maize, which was the main diet of the porters. As the safaris usually went through virgin country where there were no shops, provision had to be made at the start for sufficient food to last long periods, supplemented, of course, by meat shot along the journey.

It was an entertainment to sit on the verandah of the hotel and watch the porters run from load to load, testing each to find one lighter than the rest, and not too bulky and badly balanced. This was of some importance as each day's trek might be up to ten miles.

An American millionaire, who made a number of safaris, was Paul Rainey, who hunted lions with dogs. He employed a big game hunter called Fritz Schindler, who it was said, took drugs. The latter attempted to tweak a wounded lion's tail, but was badly mauled and was brought back to the hotel where he died. This caused a sensation as no previous example of a white hunter being mauled and killed by a lion, could be remembered. Indeed the odds are so heavily in favour of the hunter with a rifle that he is exposed to little or no danger; this is a fiction fostered by the so-called sportsman to indulge his lust for killing and his pose of being a hero.

Wild animals, it is well known, are always on the alert and will sidle away whenever they are disturbed, it is an automatic reaction. This is so, even with a lion, who will give way to a human being as has been proved by those who have encountered one face to face. The exception may be the rhino, who, being shortsighted, is liable to charge perhaps more as a precaution. Since there is no certainty in the behaviour of a wild animal, it is obviously advisable to take no chances, particularly with one that has been wounded or molested or is at bay.

The stupid Victorian idea that wild animals, as opposed to the tame variety, were dangerous, and that it was a brave, even a noble thing to kill them, has resulted in the loss to mankind of one of its greatest heritages, the beautiful and

interesting wild life now savagely depleted and almost destroyed within the last hundred years.

Many an old-timer will remember the ridiculous pose of the hero in stage plays, when he announced his intention of retiring to the wilds and hunting savage animals to prove his worth, after being thwarted in love or losing his fortune betting at the races.

This idea was further advanced by a sporting firm in London who published lists of names of people who had acquired fame for having killed superb examples of animals with a record length of tusk, horn or skin. It is incredible what a lot of harm a wrong idea can cause. Even in this more enlightened age, it is an uphill fight to prevent the habitual destroyer from hunting and killing animals wantonly.

Animals were so plentiful, their lives were considered to be of little value; everyone had a rifle, and parties of young men would ride out every weekend on their bicycles along the game tracks outside the town for a bit of sport. I had no compunction myself in doing so, but I am thankful to say that I have no recollection of shooting a single animal except for the pot, or when on safari to provide food for the native porters.

Elephant in forest, they were comparatively tame and did not run away while I was sketching

I mention here a few examples of the attitude towards the shooting of animals.

There was a gunsmith in Nairobi who regularly drove his car out on the Athi plains, where dense herds of buck and zebra were to be seen, and there he would fire into bunches of these creatures to test the penetrating power of the bullets from the rifles he had for sale. He would mention it as a recommendation that as many as three animals had been killed with a single shot, apparently he disregarded the fact that many were wounded and disabled.

A young KAR officer and his wife offered to drive a new arrival in their car to see the wild life, as a treat. Their companion sat at the back with his rifle, a normal procedure on such occasions. As they approached a little hillock beside the road, they saw a magnificent orabi standing stock still silhouetted against the sky. They slowed down, stopped the car, and as they turned to attract the attention of their guest, a shot rang out fired from his rifle and the orabi dropped dead. There was no object in this wanton destruction. It was no test of markmanship, and the carcase could not be carried away for food, nor was it of any use as a trophy. It was just left where it fell.

These two examples were from the early days and many others could be cited, but even at a later date, during the Second World War, the same idea prevailed. A young freelance hunter was given the contract to shoot buck for the food of Italian prisoners who were detained in camps dotted about the country. He boasted that within three weeks he had shot sufficient buck of all sorts, sold at a few cents a pound dead weight, to buy himself a new lorry. This slaughter continued for months and it may be estimated that many thousands of little animals were killed in this way. No wonder that the plains which once housed and fed these creatures, are now almost empty.

The wholesale disappearance of game was eventually noticed by nature lovers and slowly a reaction to the damage set in. It was realised that the animals had little or no protection; even the game wardens, whose duty it would appear to have been to protect them, would agree with the settlers that 'you cannot farm and run a game reserve.'

In Uganda it was reported that 2,000 elephants were destroyed by the game department, and that these control measures were 'conducted on the same scale as in previous years.' The unfortunate animals retreated as best they could to more inaccessible parts; north of Kenya vast herds of elephants could be seen in aerial photographs heading for the Laurien swamps, but even there they were followed up. This destruction of wild life during the last hundred years is one of the greatest crimes against nature ever perpetrated.

Nairobi in 1912

Nairobi town in the November of 1912 was little more than a village or dorp. It consisted of two main streets, Government Road which ran from the station up to the Norfolk Hotel, and Sixth Avenue, later called Delamere Avenue and now Kenyatta Avenue, which ran at right angles from a corrugated iron building called the Law Courts in the direction of 'The Hill', due west, which was the residential quarter chiefly occupied by government officials.

There was a slightly theatrical air about the place, reminiscent of a film of a gold rush from Australia or South Africa. There were few night clubs and no sheriffs about to complete the picture, but some of the types did their best by dressing the part and behaving in a rowdy manner. They usually wore top boots and riding breeches, with a pith helmet or a broad- brimmed 'double terai' hat, and across their chests a bandolier bristling with cartridges.

One young woman acquired a mild notoriety by riding her horse up and down the street one night and firing off her revolver at the electric light bulbs.

Nairobi was very advanced by having its streets lit by electricity at a time when many of the big towns in England, including parts of London, were still illuminated by gas. During the daytime the streets were a kaleidoscope of colour and variety, thronged with a motley collection of Kenya natives dressed in skins, Indians, and Somalis with their brightly-coloured shawls, all eager to satisfy their curiosity and earn an extra rupee or two, selling their beaded leather goods, wood carvings or amber necklaces.

There were also small parties of Masai moran, or warriors, whose diet consisted chiefly of drinking the blood and milk from their cattle and goats. They were very striking with their long hair in tight curls or pigtails plastered with red ochre. They wore their swords and carried spears (until this was prohibited by the authorities). As they stalked through the crowds, they were hardly noticed by other natives, although a few years earlier, until the British controlled all tribal warfare, their presence would have caused a panic amongst the Kikuyu, who were said to have feared them so much that they would scatter into the forests for protection.

Large numbers of primitive natives who wore no clothes at all were also to be seen. They shocked the Nairobians, and a regulation was quickly brought in to prohibit their entry into the township unless they wore at least a blanket. It was a difficult rule to implement and it did not solve the problem, as the unaccustomed clothing was worn more comfortably by being draped over the shoulders and back.

The really primitive native is a rarity, and is often one of nature's gentlemen. He is called a 'shenzi' which is the commonest term of abuse. The word means a barbarian or someone uncivilised, but it is indefinable, as for example, when an office boy, wishing to introduce his father and mother to the District Commissioner, asked if he might bring in two 'shenzis' to see the bwana.

My first meeting with a shenzi was on a walk outside the township while I was studying a book of Swahili phrases. Wanting to practise my vocabulary, I gave him a friendly smile. I said *'Aligani'* (greeting). He immediately held out his hand and when I put out my own, he quickly grabbed hold of my thumb. This was disconcerting. I realised that I was at his mercy and wondered what I

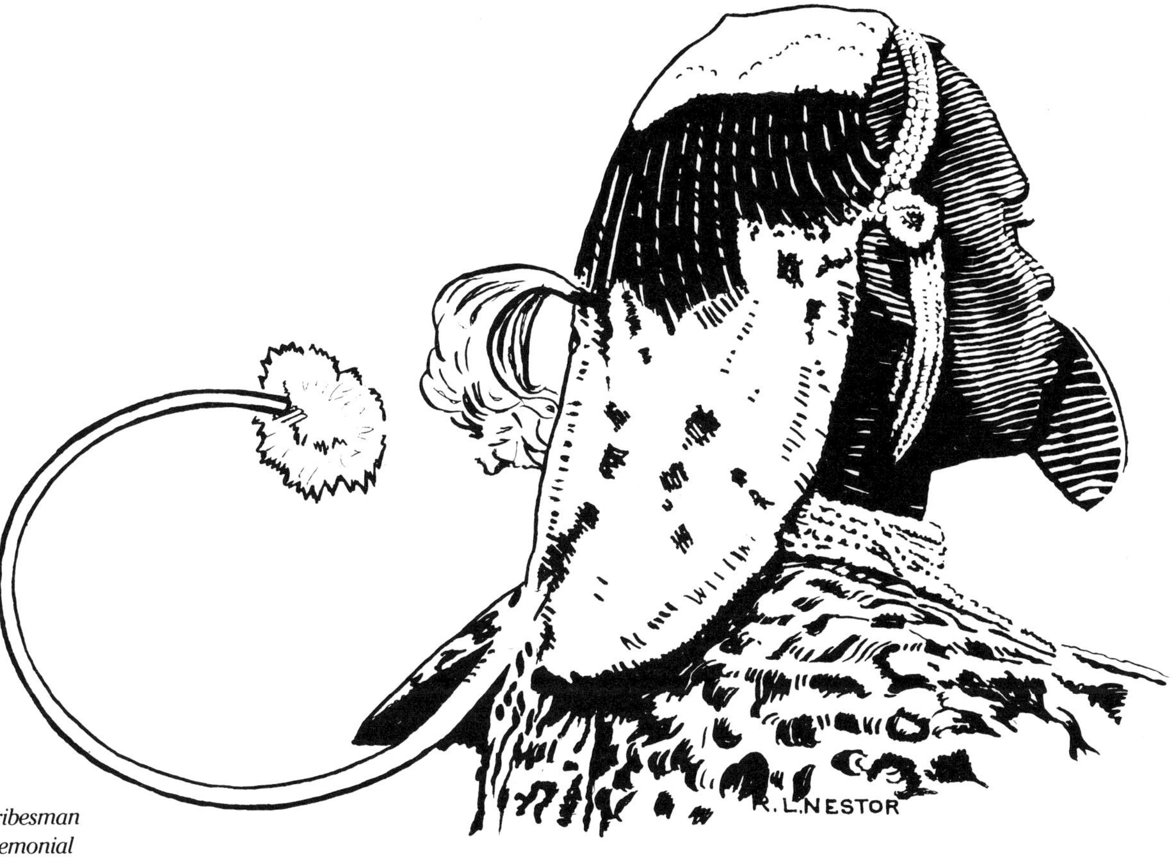

Suk tribesman in ceremonial headdress

should do next, but fortunately it was no more than a good old Kikuyu custom, and he released me to complete my part of the ceremony with a similar gesture. This was repeated two or three times till I said *'Kwa Heri'* (goodbye) and we parted.

The natives of the town were very different. They formed the basis of the servant population and were unreliable. As a general rule they were recruited directly from the streets and persuaded to take on a job without any previous experience whatsoever and so had to be trained from the start to do the simplest household duties. The salaries paid them per month were correspondingly low and in the circumstances a very low standard of service was only to be expected.

The primitive native of Kenya accepted everyone as an equal, and showed no deference or servility towards his so-called superiors, as was often the attitude of the Indians. Nairobi is in the heart of the Kikuyu country and this tribe provided the greater part of the labour supply, not only the house servants but also the unskilled jobs such as porters and ricksha boys, for public transport.

The layout of Nairobi has been a source of inconvenience and trouble since the start. This was due to the fact that there was no town planning. Roads were said to have developed originally from game tracks and they meandered deviously in all directions. The result was a jumble of irregularly shaped areas in between, which were difficult to subdivide into suitable rectangular plots for buildings and shops. Another undesirable feature was the division of the business area into an European and an Indian part in close proximity. The latter, which included the natives as well, was not only a shopping but a residential area and was a danger to the district owing to the insanitary state of the streets. As the years passed many attempts were made to buy out the Indians, and to move them to a more suitable part elsewhere, but they refused; they were too wealthy, and threatened to reverse the process and buy out the Europeans instead.

When it rained the water drained down in a deluge from the 'Hill' residential area and the lower town became a quagmire. The mud roads were often a foot deep and more in water and the traffic came to a stop. This traffic consisted of bicycles and rickshas with an occasional ox wagon. It was no uncommon sight to see a wagon drawn by a full team of sixteen working oxen being driven down Government Road.

It was a dull life for a young man fresh from the delights of London. There was little in the way of entertainment, so that many of us rode down in parties on our bicycles to the railway station to meet the trains from Mombasa, which arrived twice a week, in order to inspect the new arrivals. Alternatively, we cycled around the main streets.

I remember only three cars; the Government House car, the one provided for members of Muthaiga Club, and a run-about belonging to the Land Officer. The last was a source of entertainment to us every lunch hour, as we watched its owner attempting to start it up.

On one occasion we saw a large crowd in 6th Avenue and heard that there was a murder trial in progress. This was a very exceptional diversion and the court was thronged to capacity. It was the first trial in Kenya of a white man for murder, he was a South African of the name of Grobbelaar being tried for the murder of his wife. The trial was held in the local theatre because the accommodation in the Magistrates Court, which was at the same time the High Court, was inadequate.

It was an extraordinary proceeding. The judge was seated on the stage, with the jury scattered about either in the orchestra or on the stage, and the lawyers for the crown and the defence were grouped on each side of the judge. A touch of fantasy was introduced by the stage decorations with the gaudy backcloth and two painted masks on the pillars, depicting comedy and tragedy. The accused was unable to speak English and the trial had been delayed for over a month while an Afrikaans-speaking lawyer was found to defend him. There were also the interpreters to add to the confusion, since the meaning of each question and reply had to be repeated, explained and thrashed out to the satisfaction of all concerned.

As the young accused was proved beyond question to have shot his wife, and there were no extenuating circumstances, he was condemned to death according to the law. This presented another problem as no official hangman had been appointed.

I was told by the District Commissioner, 'Hammy' Hamilton, that unless a hangman could be procured, it was the duty of the DC himself to carry out the sentence, which at any rate, he had to supervise.

It is uncertain whether the sentence was carried out or not; it might have been

Rain at Kipkarren, rain fell in sheets and roads became impassable

the first job of a curious character known as Hangman 'Hoppy' Marshal, a white clerk in the DC's office who had a limp. In the course of time he became very proficient, and confessed that he looked upon it as routine and it worried him not at all. He was well known in Nairobi and as he was also somewhat of a comedian, and entertaining, it apparently made no difference to his social standing and he was accepted on all sides.

The two entertainments available to Nairobi audiences were the theatre and Garvies Bioscope, a term now so obsolete it seems necessary to explain that it was, of course, the name for the cinema. The bioscope films were presumably the rejects of the distributing company, as the photographs of scenes gave the impression that they were taken during a heavy shower of rain. The hall where they were shown was a disused warehouse, the seating accommodation consisted of a number of benches put together for the occasion and made of hard planks. But we enjoyed the shows all the same.

The theatre on the other hand, so we thought, was of a high standard comparable, within its limits, with that of any other to be found elsewhere in the world. I may mention, in parenthesis, that this is a common delusion of most obscure societies; as for example, when a committee member of our Kenya Arts and Crafts Society once encountered at the Royal Academy of Arts in London, remarked that it was a poor show and did not hold a candle to one of our own exhibitions! Nevertheless, our amateur dramatic society took its functions very seriously and produced some ambitious productions with conspicuous success.

At the top of 6th Avenue on a bluff of the hill overlooking the town was the site of Nairobi Club, then a wood and iron bungalow, and down a side road within a hundred yards of the club was the first house I rented with a lawyer friend. It was a shabby little wood and iron bungalow and Hodge, a QC did not remain for long, as he decided the type of work available which combined that of an advocate and solicitor was distasteful to him, but it was the normal practice in Nairobi.

This left me with a house on my own, and when my sister, Vivian, heard the news she persuaded me to allow her to come out and keep house for me.

I was astonished at the difference it made to my popularity to have a pretty young sister in tow. Many a superior young farmer, businessman and official now smarmed around and hailed me as a long lost brother. Houses of the most senior officials, previously closed to me, were now thrown open. Girls were at a premium; the proportion of men to women was about 20 to 1, so she had the time of her life. Invitations were showered on us, till I began to find them embarrassing. I was in no position to return the hospitality and entertainment we received; also I spent most of our outings merely as an escort. At dances, where I was no performer, I kicked my heels for hours until quite late into the night to take her home. Nowadays, young girls look after themselves, but at that time, such a thing would have been unthinkable.

It was therefore with some relief that I greeted the news that she had become engaged to be married.

In the meantime, she helped me to transfer to another house. It happened in this way; the head of my department, Mr Townsend, was due to take his six months' leave in England, accompanied by his wife. His government quarters had to be occupied, but all the more senior members of the Survey Department were already in houses of their own, so I, who had my sister to help me, was considered to be the most suitable choice. It was an incongruous situation and not without arousing some jealousy.

It was a large fully-furnished bungalow with numerous out-buildings in extensive grounds, in a very auspicious position situated on a road curving between the entrance gates of Government House, and a fine view down into the town. In addition there was a private ricksha with liveried attendants, fortunately included, and a charming parrot with whom I was soon on friendly terms.

The Survey Department

My first contact with the Survey Department in Nairobi was disconcerting. When I reported my arrival and presented myself for work, I was informed that they had received no instructions from England of my appointment, but it was improbable that I should have been provided with a sea passage and other privileges without good reason. There were fortunately vacancies and plenty of work available, so I was accepted without further question.

The Survey Department to which I was now attached as a computer, was divided into two parts. The first part consisted of Royal Engineers who fixed by

Triangulation the positions of prominent points on hills throughout the country. These major trig. points, as they were called, formed the framework and data for the work of the Cadastral Surveys, which formed the second part of the Survey Department. Cadastral Surveys relate to the property boundaries. And the Cadastral Survey, in its turn was further divided into two parts: the Surveyors who did the work in the field, surveying new land or subdividing where necessary, and the second part which consisted of the headquarters staff, whose job it was for the computers to check the accuracy of the surveys done by Staff Surveyors and independent licenced surveyors.

The personnel of the Survey Department, particularly the field staff, were recruited from the Colonies and Protectorates as well as from the old country. There were some from as far away as New Zealand and Australia, but the majority came from South Africa, not only because this country was the nearest but also because the system of survey adopted in Kenya was based largely on that practised in South Africa. It will be appreciated that the type of survey applicable to large open spaces differs from that required for closer work such as township areas to be found in England, although the principles of survey remain the same.

Survey work in the field often lasts for months on end, when the surveyor is cut off from contact with other white people. It is a lonely existence and one, which is often unsuitable for some who enter the profession without the experience or the capacity to endure this type of life.

We grumbled a great deal about our salaries, but in comparison with those in other employments our emoluments were fair and, in fact, generous at that time, before the First World War.

The pensions were equally liberal. An official could retire after 20 years or continue at the discretion of either party. These liberal leave and pension conditions were based on the misconception that the climate of Kenya was unhealthy, whereas experience has shown that it is practically a health resort.

It was virtually impossible for a civil servant to be dismissed. Each year the head or director made a report on the members of his department. This was usually reduced to the formula: 'Mr X. has performed his duties with diligence and fidelity and is recommended for his increment of salary.' After such a statement had been accepted for a year or two, it was difficult to prohibit the increment, without serious grounds for such an action. The result was that some passengers settled down to a routine of 'working to rule'.

The Survey Department was in its infancy when I joined, many of the staff were in their first two-and-a-half years' tour of service and slowly settling down to new conditions but looking forward to the prospect of many years of steady employment. The settlers were also recent owners of their farms, and were reaping the advantages of hard work put into the development of their virgin land with prospects of bumper crops.

The 1914–14 War

Wars and slumps are rarely heralded with warnings of the disaster to come, rather do they arrive when least expected. The sabre rattling of Kaiser Bill in Germany, and the threats and complaints bandied about on all sides, we had become accustomed to, and had accepted as a lot of hot air, but it suddenly came to a head and burst into flames.

England, we were told, was preparing for war. The wireless had not been invented and news leaked through intermittently, so, although we were excited we were not dismayed as it seemed incredible that anything could happen to us in our little backwater.

England had been at peace for so long, nobody, neither the Army, nor the authorities or the people were prepared for war. So that when it was declared in 1914, no arrangements had been made for such a contingency and great confusion resulted.

Government officials were informed that they would not be given permission to join the forces. The population of Kenya consisted almost entirely of young men in their early twenties, few were over thirty and only a small number of senior officials were over forty. This meant that permission to join the forces would have denuded the population of workers, and would have brought the machinery of the country to a standstill.

However, large numbers of young farmers and those in employments in shops and offices descended on Nairobi expecting to be enrolled in some military unit without delay, for which no provision had been made. The limited accommodation of the town was quite unable to cope with the inflow. Hotels were overcrowded and food was scarce. Much of the enthusiasm evaporated under these conditions and most of the young men returned reluctantly to their occupations until later arrangements were made to enrol them.

Early in 1915 I had completed my 30 months' tour of service in the Government and was due for my five months' return leave in England.

England, 1915

On my arrival in England the excitement of the war was in full swing. Everywhere young men were to be seen in khaki, and I naturally felt conspicuous. Those of us in our 'civvies' were not unlikely to be handed a white feather by young women who were very disapproving, and I had to explain on many occasions that I could not get permission to join up as I was a Kenya Government official. This explanation was not accepted with any enthusiasm.

In the meantime, I booked in at a private hotel in the Cromwell Road and had the experience one night of seeing the first Zeppelin from Germany being shot down over London. The huge sausage-shaped dirigible balloon was quite clearly visible to the eye, as were the ineffectual shells fired at it, but it was attacked by an aeroplane and shot down in flames. The airman received one of the first VC's of the war.

It was not long before the indignity of being a civilian and having to endure the belittling glances of my acquaintances, drove me to ask permission to join up. But this was refused by the Colonial Office, who informed me that every available young man was urgently needed to defend the country of Kenya, where the war was also in progress.

I had already experienced the discomfort of the first two-and-a-half months of my leave, and had started on my 'return leave' granted on the understanding that I should be returning to Kenya for duty. But I found the situation unbearable, and submitted my resignation which was accepted with the warning that I might not be re-engaged in the event of my applying for my job at a future date; and I was also to refund the amount of 'return' salary I had been paid. This did not appear to be a serious risk in view of the uncertainties of life in the future.

Joining-up

So, in the circumstances it was inevitable that I should volunteer for one of the Services, and I submitted my application to the war office. There must be innumerable motives behind the urge to join up in the event of war. Patriotism is one of these, but in many cases by no means the most important. The herd instinct is equally urgent, to do what is expected of one and join one's age group, or a sense of adventure and a relief from the humdrum boredom of ordinary life. Very few healthy young men expect or are afraid they will be killed, although there are certainly some who suffer such a premonition, and nevertheless take the risk. There is undoubtedly a great deal of pleasure in the companionship of other young men; the interest of being taught and the competence which it engenders, the responsibility, even the pleasure of wearing a uniform, and the approval of our relatives and acquaintances, particularly the young women among them, for doing what is considered to be the right thing; all these encourage recruiting.

I had made numerous attempts to join the Royal Engineers, for which I was best qualified, but was informed that there was already too long a waiting list. I therefore applied for the Artillery instead where the young recruiting officer, on hearing that I was an engineer, immediately accepted my application for the RE and I was instructed to report to the Officers' Training Corps at the Inns of Court, where all recruits were taught to drill and give commands.

But first, there was the pleasure of ordering my uniform at one of the best tailors in London. This included riding breeches, top boots and spurs as well as a Sam Browne belt. It was all very exciting and somewhat like a fancy dress party. For this extravagance my father and uncle each contributed £50, as at that time we were given no uniform allowance as officers.

France

Before long we were ordered to France, first to Rouen, where we remained for a week or two, awaiting our orders to proceed to the front. All information of our movements was kept very secret, even from ourselves. We did not know when we were to be moved, nor to what part of the line we were to be sent. We got our orders to pack and to embark on a particular train at a moment's notice. At some stop midway, we were turned out to sit on the platform for an hour or more, till we were hustled into another train. And so in the course of time we arrived at the terminus, as near the front line as was permitted. Here we heard the first sounds of heavy gunfire.

A car delivered me to the headquarters of my Company which was at Bacodel Becour, near Fricourt on the Somme, and I reported to my OC, Major B.S. Philpot of the 97th Field Company, of the 21st Division of the 3rd Army.

Here my OC took me up one day to test my reactions under gunfire. It was a wet day and we rode up to as near as was convenient to the front line, where we left our horses. I was amused to find that I not only had a better horse than my OC, but that my mount insisted on remaining in the lead, splashing the Major and his horse with the wet mud he threw up behind with his hoofs. I tried my best to hold him, but in spite of many irritable commands from my OC to get to the rear, he would seize every opportunity to slip into the lead. I learnt later that 'Khaki', as he was called, had been the OC's horse, and had been passed down through the more senior ranks till I, as the most junior subaltern, had him allotted to me. The reason for this was because 'Khaki' was said to have a bad habit of dipping or stumbling and throwing his rider, but I was lucky not to have this experience with him.

My first experience in the front line was not very terrifying. It had just been under heavy gunfire, but it was over, and the only thing that impressed me was a strong smell, rather like garlic or onions.

While we marked time at company headquarters, preparing for the First Battle of the Somme, we had many odd jobs to do, the most boring of which was the censoring of letters of the sappers of our own sections, to their relatives or friends in England. Our OC, Major Philpot, reminded us that we must cross out any reference or description which could enable the enemy to locate our position at the front.

'But what can we say?' we asked.

'You can say that there are some fine willow trees here,' he said. 'The willow grows profusely all over this part'.

As it happened, this was probably the most enlightening description of our whereabouts for the enemy; since the stream passing between Fricourt and Becodel, was clearly marked 'Willow Stream' on all the maps of the district. The result of these rigid restrictions on the correspondence reduced the pattern of most letters to the formula:

'Dear Ma, I hope this finds you in the pink, as it leaves me at present.'

The First Battle of the Somme

There has been so much written about the horrors of war, that there is not much that can be added. Mostly one is reminded of a series of pictures of shell holes, stumps of trees, barbed wire, ammunition dumps, trenches full of mud and water with duckboards, white chalk.

The noise was continuous, and if it stopped for ten seconds it immediately attracted one's attention. It has been remarked, and it is no exaggeration, that a sudden lull would awaken one out of a deep sleep.

One soon got accustomed to it so that only trivial things impressed themselves on one's memory. For example, the sight of lovely red poppies shining in the white chalk forming a scarlet and green arch against the sky as one walked along the sunken trench, was an unfailing source of wonder and delight.

One day, in the system of trenches I passed a deep dug-out, from which there issued the sweetest music I thought I had ever heard. I had to bend down and listen between bursts of intermittent gunfire. It was a gramophone, playing a popular melody called 'Bird of love divine'.

On dark nights, and we usually worked at night after 'stand to' at 6pm, the sudden illumination from a burst of Very lights in the sky, like beautiful fireworks, would light up the dismal scene of no man's land. Dark shadows of hillocks would stand out, with bare tree stumps and barbed wire. The whole scene would be illuminated for a few seconds as light as day. On two separate occasions, I saw dogs bounding along towards us from the direction of the German front line, and I wondered whether they were carrying messages, and if we should try to intercept them.

The trenches were not continuous stretches, but were broken every ten or twenty feet with traverses, or right-angular deviations, as a protection against the effect of bursting shells. They had steps on which one could stand to look over the top. The trenches had names such as Piccadilly Circus and Regent Street, or Dead Horse Corner. One particularly dangerous salient in our front line was called the Tambour. It had a sinister sound but was probably only the French for a drum. Another unpleasant lot of trenches ran through Fricourt cemetery, where gunfire had opened up many of the graves.

My own dug-out, marked with a large RE, was in a hollow about half-a-mile back from the front line. Many a time at night, I would be disturbed with loud knocking on the door, with an urgent request that I should come at once as the wire entanglements had been cut. But what could I do? Only turn round and try and get to sleep again as best I could with the rats racing over my bed, till I collected a piece of chalk and hurled it in the direction of the sound of scampering feet.

In front of my dug-out, which was in a hollow, as I have said, there was a level stretch, and then a road leading westward to La Boisselle. On this level stretch, every day the casualties were laid out with their heads and bodies covered with gunny bags. One would have expected that there were enough gruesome sights without these pitiful objects, yet it was an unfailing attraction for some ghouls, who could be seen passing up and down the lines of prostrate forms. They would lift the bags and shout out to their companions. 'Here! Have a look at this one'.

In the trenches preparation for 'D' day was intensified. The days passed and our shelling became more and more heavy. It was said that there was one gun to every yard of the line: probably a great exaggeration. 'D' day arrived and the push started. The casualties were considered to be the heaviest during the war. Sheets of *The Times* and *Daily Telegraph* were filled with closely-printed names of the dead and wounded. It was said that at the height of the advance, there were as many as ten thousand casualties in one day.

Luckily for me, I was wounded early in this First Battle of the Somme in July 1916. It was a curious experience. I was standing in a group of sappers of my RE Section, when a six-inch shell landed in among us. Up to 20 casualties resulted. I was on the fringe of the group and therefore protected from the full impact. As is well known, if one hears a shell arriving, one is safe. I did not hear this one. My first knowledge of the event was to find myself in a trench, where I had been taken for cover. Here I found my face and clothes drenched with blood. Splinters from the shell had hit me in the head. The artery in my left temple had been severed and the blood kept spouting out with each pulse beat. The real danger was bleeding to death, as, at that time, there was no blood transfusion service available. Other splinters cut a furrow down my cheek below the eye, and another nearly removed my ear. Altogether it was a very lucky escape.

I felt no pain, that was to come later with the dressings, but as I was literally light-headed, I found myself, at intervals, shouting at the top of my voice as though I were very drunk. All very disturbing in a room full of wounded and dying. How I reached the advanced dressing station I never discovered, but there must have been transport nearby. At the advance dressing station my wounds were dressed and the artery plugged. And I found myself in an ambulance, with many others, bound for the railway station and the train to take us to No. 2 Red Cross Hospital at Rouen. Here I was expertly dressed and sown up by a surgeon – Austin – whose name I still remember.

Some of my sappers were there also, and they asked for me. It was pathetic to see the pride with which they kept large pieces of shell from their wounds as mementos. Souvenirs of an experience which they may never have lived to remember.

Back to England

We were hurriedly evacuated from this hospital to make room for the relays of casualties arriving. First, we were ferried across the Channel to Southampton and there we caught the Red Cross train to London. It was in this that I first realised the advantage of my spectacular appearance as a wounded soldier. My wounds were not serious, but in my blood-stained uniform with my head swathed in bandages, I certainly caught the eye.

As we travelled, an officer passed along the corridor handing out tickets for the hospitals to which we were to go. I remembered the advice I had been given 'If wounded ask for Park Lane', which I did.

'Oh, no,' he said, 'I have only two tickets for 17 Park Lane,' and he walked away.

Shortly after, back he came. 'You the fellow who asked for Park Lane?' he said, eyeing my bandages, 'You may as well have them'. So I, and my neighbour, got away with it, and it was indeed a great stroke of luck.

A new, exciting and interesting life now opened up for me. On our arrival at Charing Cross Station, huge crowds of sightseers lined the platforms, and filled the courtyard into the Strand. We were cheered and flowers were showered on us. A Rolls-Royce was there to take us to the hospital at 17 Park Lane, and we generally received VIP treatment as never before. Here, while in bed, my relatives brought me a *Daily Mirror* of 5 July 1916, where I was astonished to see a photograph of myself, with this caption 'Second Lt. Nestor is reported wounded'. How it got into the paper I never discovered, perhaps it was submitted by Lefayette, the Bond Street photographers, where I had been photographed.

Sir Alfred Fripp, the famous surgeon to the Queen and Consultant at Guy's Hospital, was in charge of the hospital in 17 Park Lane. He remarked to the students who accompanied him on his tours of inspection, how well the surgeon at Rouen had patched up my wounds, particularly those on the face and head. The VADs were well-known society beauties, such as Diana Manners and Violet de Trafford and Eleanor Glynn's red-haired daughter was the theatre nurse.

From 17 Park Lane, we went next door to Londonderry House to convalesce. Here, I was very much envied as a young girl masseuse sat on the side of my bed and massaged my face in full view of the whole ward.

Sir Alfred Fripp arranged for three of us, his patients from Londonderry House, to attend a 'Souvenir Lunch' at Grosvenor House, belonging to the Duke of Westminster, which was to be demolished, and made into the hotel of that name. The house was very much in the same state as it was when in occupation, with the pictures on the walls and the furniture in position. The famous *Blue Boy* by Gainsborough was still there, before it was sold and removed to America.

Patients did not remain for long in London, as the accommodation was limited, and Sir Alfred Fripp arranged for three or four of us to go to Polesden Lacey, the home near Dorking of the Hon. Mrs Ronald Greville, a friend of his. It was a great privilege and experience for many of us who would never otherwise have had the opportunity to live in the many magnificent private houses which were thrown open to the wounded soldiers; nor was this privilege repeated to the same extent in World War II.

It was a most delightful place to convalesce, but unfortunately my health did not improve, and a more bracing climate was considered to be advisable, so I was transfered to Cromer on the East Coast.

Overstrand Hall at Cromer was an almost equally luxurious house surrounded by extensive grounds including a miniature golf course. It belonged to Sir Derrick and Lady Keppel. He was Comptroller to the Household of HM the King. Our kind host and hostess accepted us as members of the family, and took us round to see their friends in the neighbourhood, known as the Dukeries. The contents of all these beautiful houses gave me a new interest, that of antiques, and inspired me many years later, to take a course of Chinese art and Archaeology at the Courtauld Institute under Professor Howard Hansford; and still later, when in South Africa, to start a society known as the Antiques Study Circle, which soon collected a membership of over 300 and to which I was elected Hon. Life President.

From what I have written, it will be appreciated that wounded soldiers during the First World War were extremely well-treated. And I look back with gratitude to the generous treatment I received. The state of my disabilities did not improve, and the remainder of my time in the army was divided by spells of light duty at Newark, one of the RE depots, and various convalescent homes and hospitals; but no return to active service in France.

Sir Alfred Fripp advised me that I must report to him regularly, and in 1917 he performed a number of operations on me at Guy's Hospital. After this I was sent to Bournemouth and to 'Sandacres', a house belonging to Sir Ernest Cassel, but I had the choice of being sent to any part of England, or the South of France. Georgina, Countess of Dudley, was in charge of the arrangements in London for sending officers to convalescent homes, and they were instructed to apply to her. She was affectionately known as 'old Georgina', and on one occasion in Kenya when a number of us were discussing the war, I referred to her by this familiar name. But I was somewhat taken aback when one of my listeners pulled out a photograph from his pocket and said, 'My mother'. He was Captain the Hon. Cyril Ward, RN.

My last convalescent home was Mont D'Or in Bournemouth, from where I was invalided out of the Army with a small gratuity and pension, and the bleak prospect of having to look for a job. The maximum 100 per cent disability pension for a captain was £210 per annum.

The war was still on, and as pilots for the Flying Corps were badly needed, I thought I might be able to work an acceptance. But I could not pass the medical tests; the first of which consisted of standing on one leg and shutting my eyes, when I immediately lost my balance. The doctor said: 'It would be criminal on my part and suicidal on yours'. And so I bethought of my old job in Kenya.

Kenya after the Armistice

After the Armistice, which was celebrated with great enthusiasm in London, I obtained my passage by sea back to Kenya, via South Africa. On arrival at Mombasa I found the country in a turmoil.

The Indian Question

The Indians, many of whom had been in Kenya from as early as 1897, when they were brought in to help to build the Uganda Railway, demanded equal political rights with the Europeans, no segregation, rights to hold land in the highlands, and promotion to the highest ranks in the Civil Service. The Europeans, on the other hand, pointed out that this meant the end of white settlement, as the Indians outnumbered the whites by 2 to 1.

The Home Government appeared to approve the Indian demands, so the Kenya Europeans declared that they would fight for their rights. We learnt that a War Council had been summoned with a General and staff at its head, and it was estimated that they had the support of at least 1,000 ex-soldiers. It is not known whether the Kings African Rifles was expected to join them. Plans were drawn up to capture the Treasury, Railway and Postal Departments. Senior officals were to be arrested and the governor kidnapped and removed to a remote farm.

It was, of course, a half-baked project, since they were a ridiculously small and ill-equipped force, and the country was far from being self-supporting. Necessary supplies could easily be stopped by blockading the port of Mombasa. However, the Indians were eventually given five seats in the Legislative Council to the Europeans' eleven. The Secretary of State affirmed that Kenya was an African territory and HM Government recorded their considered opinion, that 'the interests of the African native must be paramount'. It was a very important decision and not very acceptable to the white settlers, but the threat of a rebellion came to an end.

The Harry Thuku Riot

Nevertheless, the underlying discontent continued, not only among the Indians, but also among some of the more educated natives. The leader of the latter was Harry Thuku, Secretary of the Young Kikuyu Association who claimed to represent his tribe and asserted their support to the Indian demands. This, however, was repudiated by Kinanjui, the paramount chief of the Kikuyu. Thuku continued to stir up trouble – so much so that the Goanese people, of whom there were large numbers in Nairobi, became alarmed, and an amusing situation arose when they approached the 'rebel General' of the settlers, General Wheatley, and appealed to him to give orders, in the event of any active assault on the Indians, to prevent the Goanese from being attacked. As a safeguard they proposed to put a cross on the doorways of their houses.

Eventually, in the interests of law and order, Thuku was arrested and confined at the headquarters of the Police in Government Road, until suitable arrangements could be made to transport him to Lamu, an isolated port on the coast north of Mombasa.

Four of us, including the Nairobi resident magistrate, Doorley, were playing bridge that night at Nairobi Club, when he was called away to the 'phone. We waited for a long time, surprised at the delay, until he eventually returned and said he must leave as he had to go to the main police station in the town to read the riot act. Large numbers of natives had congregated in the main streets and an ugly situation was developing.

The following morning, when we left the club to go to work at our offices in the town, all the native staff had deserted. We found very large crowds of natives blocking the whole area around the police headquarters in Government Road, where Thuku had been locked up prior to his proposed deportation at 12 o'clock to the railway station, on his way to Lamu. With the greatest difficulty we managed to push our bicycles through the dense crowds to the office, which was situated almost opposite to the corrugated iron building, with its corrugated iron fence which served as police headquarters.

We had a grandstand view from our front offices. It was interesting to watch the crowd and the stupidity of many Europeans, who insisted on mingling with the rioters, even accompanied by their children. Motorists also tried, until they were stopped by the police, to barge their way through the crowds, which completely filled the streets from far past the Norfolk Hotel to the Jevanjee Gardens, a distance of about half-a-mile, and also along the side streets and in the adjoining open spaces.

Immediately below our office windows the crowd was seated 30 deep. A good half of them where Kikuyu women, who every now and then broke into a curious whinnying noise, 'te, te, te' it sounded like; and this appeared to inflame the anger of their menfolk, most of whom were armed with sticks and knob kerries. We were surprised to see one of the ring-leaders was a member of the Red Cross, judging from his uniform and the hat he wore with initials on it. He walked up and down harangueing the crowd. And across the street the famous American big game photographers and writers, Martin and Osa Johnson, were to be seen, dodging about to find a good vantage point for their ciné cameras. Nobody appeared to be alarmed. We, in our office, watched the proceedings expectantly and calmly, but we took the precaution of arming ourselves with axe shafts from the store.

The situation had remained unchanged for some hours, and we were considering the problem of returning to our homes for lunch, when all of a sudden there was a scuffle, the crowds surged backwards and forwards and there was a burst of gunfire. The first volley seemed to have been fired into the air, and we realised it was ball cartridge that was used, as it struck the branches of the trees, but the firing continued. Immediately panic ensued. The crowd scattered in all directions, men and women, dressed in their skins, tried to take cover in our office rooms, and some succeeded in forcing their way in, in spite of our fight to keep them out. They ran through the buildings to the back, and so away to safety.

But the great majority ran down the street, jostling and knocking each other down. Some collapsed as they were shot in the back. One of the excitable members of our white staff grabbed a loaded rifle he had handy and was taking aim, when he was stopped in time, otherwise he would certainly have committed murder. Very soon the crowds cleared. A party of armed askaris headed by a white officer, marched down the streets, and we went out to view the scene. A number of casualties, dead and wounded, or hurt, lay about and on a tree a man who had been shot, was sticking in the fork.

We learnt afterwards that the outbreak of firing had all been unpremeditated. Apparently an elderly police officer had opened the gate in the corrugated fence around the police station and had stumbled, or had been tripped, and the native askari on guard at the gate became alarmed and opened fire without orders. This started a general fusillade which could not be easily controlled.

My friend Doorley told me that a small native 'toto' was brought before him accused of causing the trouble by trying to slip between the legs of the elderly police officer. He was so small he could hardly peer over the rail of the dock in court. So he was discharged. Small matters can cause such serious catastrophies. This was the first major indication of the 'Wind of Change' which was to blow we knew not where.

The Soldier Settlement Scheme

When I first arrived in Kenya in 1912 there were about 5,000 whites in the country.

The population of Europeans in 1900:	3,175
The population of Europeans in 1921:	9,651
The population of Europeans in 1931:	16,812
The population of Europeans in 1937:	18,000 approximately

The white population of the country was greatly increased by the introduction of the 'right type of settler', who participated in the Soldier Settlement Scheme, and as many of them brought their war gratuities and other capital, this gave the finances a fictitious aspect of prosperity, and introduced the insidious snare of inflation, with its attendant high prices and discontent.

The Soldier Settlement Scheme of 1919 was one of the most important events in the history of Kenya. It was launched with the object of increasing white settlement, and at the same time providing home and employment for discharged soldiers after the war. It also had the merit of developing large areas of what was considered to be vacant farm land, to provide the raw materials so necessary for the industrial progress of the motherland, England. Superficially, it appeared to be an excellent idea, but the chief danger lay in the ignorance of

Thika Falls, Elspeth Huxley lived near here as a child, 'The Flame Trees of Thika' is set in this area

RAY NESTOR

many, perhaps most, of the participants in farming knowledge and practice. Nor did it take into account the attitude of some who had grandiose ideas and considered their farms to be 'hunting boxes'. With this object in view they spent the greater part of their capital building themselves comfortable houses, which the practical farmer would generally leave to the last.

But there were numerous other factors which mitigated against the success of the scheme. The authorities had not taken into account the suitability of certain areas for the growing of crops envisaged, whether it be coffee, maize, sisal, tea or mixed farming; nor were the officers of the agricultural department sufficiently experienced to advise on the type of farming they had to supervise. This was unknown virgin country.

Briefly the scheme provided for two types of settlers. Those who could show proof that they had sufficient capital to buy their farms, at very advantageous rates, and develop them; these were the B-farmers. And secondly the A-farmers, who were expected to have enough capital to make a reasonable living without the expense of buying their farms. The areas of the B-farms varied from about 500 acres up to 2,000 to 3,000 acres according to the proportion of arable land and the situations of the land. Whereas the A-farms consisted of land selected as economic units, of approximately 160 acres, i.e. a quarter of a square mile, containing a high proportion of arable land suitable for valuable crops, such as coffee.

Applicants for both A- and B-farms were asked to submit a series of farm numbers, in the order of their choice, as there would naturally be many applicants for the better farms. And these were then included in a raffle. If you were lucky enough to have your name drawn early, you got one of the first choices on your list. And the chances of getting a farm were very good indeed, as there were hardly enough applicants for the hundreds of free A-farms available.

Most of the junior officials applied for the A-farms, but applicants were by no means confined to Kenya residents; many young men and women, formerly in the forces in England, also applied and drew farms in the raffle. Indeed the object of the scheme was to encourage new settlers, and the majority of the B-farmers were new arrivals chiefly from England, but also from New Zealand, Australia and the other colonies. Syndicates were formed of three or more people, and in some cases they obtained as much as 10,000 acres.

Safari to Ithanga

One of my first jobs on returning to Kenya was to join a party to survey the 'Ithanga Farms' for the Soldier Settlement Scheme. The area to be divided into 160 acre A-farms at Ithanga, near Thika, was about 15 to 20 miles east of Nairobi. For the safari we had to recruit over 100 porters, with whom we walked as well, since there was no other transport. Their job was to carry not only our survey equipment, tents, bedding and personal belongings, but also large numbers of bags of 'posho' or mealie-meal, for their own food and for the other porters, as there were few shops along the route where food for the porters could be bought. The load for a porter was 40 to 60 lbs, and we usually marched about ten miles a day.

The Kavarondo tribe made the best porters, they were of better physique than

Malindi road

the Kikuyu, and some of them took a pride in carrying the heaviest loads, and racing ahead to arrive at our camp site first. Once we started work and pitched camp, they had a good long rest. We pitched our tents as near to whatever water supply we found convenient, and worked during the mornings and evenings, resting during the heat of the day.

But we also had time to go shooting guinea fowl and francolin for the pot, using .22 rifles. There was no difficulty in keeping ourselves well supplied as the flocks were very numerous. One day, I disturbed a snake and was surprised to see it glide away on top of the dry grass, instead of underneath it as one would expect. Snakes are very rarely responsible for the death of human beings in Kenya; unlike India where tens of thousands are killed every year. The natives are more vulnerable as they walked bare-footed. I have known of only two cases of snake bite of Europeans, neither of which was fatal.

This camp site was very unhealthy, the sides of the tent and our mosquito nets were festooned with mosquitoes that hung in rows from the material. One way of partially clearing them was to hold the chimney of a lighted kerosene lamp below and watch them drop into the flame.

It was not long before some of us got bouts of high fever. The nearest government doctor was at Fort Hall some seven or eight miles away; we reported our illness and he sent back a bottle of quinine with instructions to take three tablets every four hours. The remedy was more drastic than the disease, and we had to return to Nairobi.

Survey lines were cut through native bean 'shambas' and other cultivation. This land was being allotted to the Soldier Settlement Scheme. The natives were not unreasonably resentful, though at that time they did not realise that the land was being taken from them. At a later date, they retaliated by pulling out the survey beacon, and on one occasion stole a theodolite.

It was a thrilling experience of that safari to hear the roar of the lions that circled around our tents at night. This was the most majestic and glorious sound imaginable, in its own appropriate surroundings. It remains in my memory as the essence of Africa.

Forest at Kipkarren,
The buck on our farm were very tame as we never shot at them

My A-farm

I joined the Soldier Settlement Scheme and drew a 160 acre A-farm at Kibigori, within two stations of the railway terminus, not one of the most fortunate situations, as it was low lying and in a very hot part of the country near Lake Victoria. But the soil was very rich, and the greater part was arable. Five of us decided to form a syndicate and grow maize or sugar cane, as there was a factory being built for the latter and we were advised that our cane would find a ready sale. This was later discovered to be a fallacy.

Like most syndicates of people who were strangers to each other, the enterprise was not a success. The partners did not always agree on plans for expenditure and development, and failed to pay their share of the expense, and the work 'hung fire', to such an extent that, one by one they decided to 'throw in their hands' and offer their shares for sale. I was satisfied that the whole area would make a good farming venture and bought out the others for less than one pound per acre, and so acquired over 800 acres. But I was over-optimistic. As I was permanently stationed in Nairobi, I could not supervise operations and had to rely upon my young Afrikaans manager, who had very little farming experience except for growing maize. However, this crop promised the best results, and I decided to start work without delay, and plow and plant 50 to 100 acres before the rains began.

My manager bought a team of working oxen at the farm, and I purchased all the necessary implements in Nairobi. I impressed on the firm I obtained them from, to dispatch everything without delay. But weeks passed and my manager wrote complaining that he had not received the goods, till eventually it was too late to attempt planting a crop before the rains. This was the first of many setbacks. Months passed and my manager, who had recently got married, found that the climate was very unhealthy, as he wrote and told me 'here are mosquitoes very bad'. Eventually, I never got a crop of any kind off the land, which was a complete loss as a farming venture. My friends in the office delighted in reminding me that 'you can't farm from the office chair'.

However, I was not deterred by this failure, for which there seemed to be many reasonable excuses. Kenya was a farming country, and the advantages of indulging in some form of farming enterprise was extolled on all sides. There were many glowing accounts of profits to be made quite easily, particularly from coffee. And besides there was the promise of a good healthy life, in beautiful surroundings, when the time for retirement should come.

It sounded to be, and was, too good to be true. The fact that coffee was a long-term crop and took no less than seven years to come to full maturity, was not stressed. Nor was it appreciated that prices fluctuated wildly, that labour was difficult and scarce, especially as all the coffee crops matured at the same time on farms adjoining each other and there were not sufficient pickers, unless one had a large area to accommodate squatters who ruined the land. Furthermore the innumerable diseases coffee was subject to, its hordes of pests, and its vulnerability to hail and erosion, were not fully understood, even by the Agricultural Department. Finally, there was the fact, that most of the land was unsuitable for coffee. The country had not been in occupation long enough to provide reliable information on the above mentioned questions, and many other points very necessary to the success of the prospective farmer. Those of us who blindly ventured into this morass were the true pioneers of the land. And there were many tragedies.

Upper Kipkarren

I decided to grow coffee and bought another two 160 acre A-farms at Upper Kipkarren in the Uasin Gishu district, some 25 miles from Eldoret township. The first of these farms was won in the raffle by the Chief of Police, who was at the time acting as Governor, and I ascertained from the reports in the Survey Department that the land was considered to be as good as that of any of the A-farms in the scheme, and eminently suitable for coffee. So I bought it for £50, the price asked.

The second farm which was unfortunately not adjoining but was within a quarter-of-a-mile from it, was owned by an acquaintance who had been transferred to West Africa and was anxious to sell it. I offered him £10 for the 160 acres which he gladly accepted.

The two were both excellent little farms at an altitude of approximately 6,000 feet. The soil was deep rich red loam up to 20 feet deep, and the land of the first farm sloped gently to a permanent stream in thickly-wooded groves. The second farm had the disadvantage of being divided by a swampy water course but was, nevertheless, a gift at the price.

All this I discovered on my first visit, when I also learnt that my properties were rather in 'the blue' and inaccessible. The branch line from Nakuru to Eldoret had not been built. The main Uganda Railway line terminated at Kisumu on Lake Victoria, a distance of some 50 miles over a steep escarpment to Kipkarren. I therefore had to hire a car from one of the intermediate stations up to Eldoret, from where I travelled by mule cart to my farm over some of the worst roads, if they could be so described, in the world. They were, in fact, chiefly water courses full of deep gullies and pig-holes which threatened to overturn our cart at any moment.

Left on my own to look over my property I shall never forget the feeling of proud possession. This was the first time I had ever owned any land and I was delighted with everything; the beauty of the scene, with the warm clean wind gently blowing over the long dry grass, the little river down below surrounded by a dense fringe of indigenous forest in which the colobus monkeys could be seen jumping from branch to branch. The stone I sat on was my own stone and the guinea fowl, calling to each other, were my own fowls.
I sat there a long time feeling very happy and fit, as I always did on my farm in Kipkarren. It was a very healthy place where the air was clean and pure without any dust, and the dry brown grass represented the essence of Kenya and of Africa for me, ever after. It was so very peaceful, without any sign or sound of a motor car or other discordant noise.

One of the chief objects of the first visit was to look around for a manager to plow up the land and plant the coffee. It was a forlorn hope, as I was to be in the neighbourhood for only a week, and had little or no contact with anyone who was likely to be suitable. After this long lapse of time I am horrified at the extent of my foolishness, and the casual attitude to what was a very important matter for me, because I recklessly engaged the first man I came across. This was a young Afrikaner, whom we saw occupied with his father-in-law, building a stone house on one of the other A-farms. He accepted the job with alacrity, and I made arrangements with a lawyer in Eldoret to draw up a contract to buy a team of oxen and the implements required.
My manager plowed up and planted 20 acres with coffee seedlings bought from

Dense forest

an adjoining farm. The acreage was increased by a further 40 acres, making a total of 60 acres of coffee which was my target. After 18 months or so, I got my first 'fly' picking of two tons of coffee, and felt that I was well on my way to fortune. What was more encouraging, the consignment contained a high percentage of first-grade coffee. The firm in Nairobi, where my parchment coffee was hulled, informed me that it was as good as the best consignment received by them that year, and I was paid the top price of £100 per ton. But that was the last I ever got with the exception of a few bags. Every year I got letters to say, there was a fine flowering with expectations of a good crop, but it never materialised. When the slump came, my white manager gave notice that he wanted an advance in wages or he would leave. I reluctantly accepted the latter demand and left the farm in charge of my native headman. I learnt later that my manager had been in the habit of selling bags of coffee in Eldoret, without my permission. He could not easily get another job, owing to the slump, and he got into trouble and committed suicide.

It has been claimed that the Soldier Settlement Scheme was a success; Elspeth Huxley states that it was estimated that 75 per cent of the settlers had made good, and were still settled on the land after eight years. This might have applied to the B-farmers with sufficient land to accommodate squatters, and so ensure their labour supply, but there is no doubt that very few, if any, of the 50 or more A-farmers in Kipkarren made a living by farming.

Nairobi town centre as it was when we were there, the mosque is in the centre

Nairobi Life

A highlight of Nairobi social life was the exhibition of paintings, under the auspices of the Kenya Arts and Crafts Society. A number of us formed the first committee, and a constitution and bye-laws were drawn up with the help of our Hon. Legal Adviser, Dacre Shaw. Exhibitions were generally held in the Memorial Hall, and there was a brisk sale of pictures, chiefly water colours and oils, of Kenya views. The Duchess of Gloucester, then Lady Alice Scott, was a regular exhibitor before her marriage and later became a patron of the Society. Another well-known personality, who exhibited his pictures with the Society, was Lord Baden-Powell, famous as the founder of the Scout movement, he was particularly interested in depicting big game.

In the first exhibition in the early 1920s, I had a portrait accepted of the Hon. Berkeley Cole. It was a pencil and chalk drawing, and I showed my sitter dressed with a red Somali shawl over his shoulders, which at that time was a fashion in Nairobi among the young settlers, such as 'Boy' Caswell Long, one of the handsomest men ever seen in Kenya.

Lord Delamere was pleased with my portrait of his brother-in-law Berkeley, and offered to buy the picture, but I had done it as a commission for the Muthaiga Club, so Lord Delamere arranged to have it reproduced by the Medici Society in London.

The Muthaiga Club

The success of this first portrait led to my receiving a commission to do a number of prominent members of Muthaiga Club, and these are still on the walls of the Members' Room at Muthaiga Club. The portraits included those of Lord Delamere, Col. Ewart Grogan, Hon. Berkeley Cole, Hon. Denys Finch-Hatton, Capt. F. O. B. Wilson, Marcus Maxwell, Frank Joyce, W. C. Hunter – for many years President of the Club, and others. A pencil portrait, from life, of Lord Francis Scott was later graciously accepted by his niece, the Duchess of Gloucester.

Muthaiga Country Club is perhaps the most famous English club outside England. It has numbered royalty as well as the aristocracy and American millionaires among its members. The members list is said to read like pages of Debrett or Burkes Peerage.

So much has been written criticising the way of life of the white people of Kenya, that a comment on this aspect of their existence may not be out of place. It has been asserted that there was considerable 'wife swapping, drinking and stripping' in which they were supposed to indulge. It is probable that there were isolated examples which gained considerable publicity because of the social standing of the people involved.

Some of the glossy magazines in England made a feature of reporting the activities of Kenya residents, because of the glamour of their personalities as members of the aristocracy, or because they had acquired a publicity value for some reason. It has often been remarked 'the British people dearly love a lord', and at that time it was certainly true. People in England rarely encountered a lord, but in Kenya they were surprisingly plentiful.

There were some, who were married or divorced several times, but no more often than many film stars of today. Lady Idina, née Sackville, had as many as seven husbands. She belonged to the famous family who lived at Knole, the stately home in Kent. Lady Idina's first husband was Capt. Charles Gordon, and when they were divorced and she married the Hon. Jocelyn Hay, later Lord Erroll, Gordon proposed Hay for the club, and lent them his house in Kenya, which was considered to be somewhat complacent and amusing, but that was all. Karen (the Baroness von) Blixen, the authoress of *Out of Africa,* was supposed to have the Hon. Denys Finch-Hatton as her boyfriend, but there was no proof of it, and it was not paraded about. It was suggested to me, that as many of these people were personally known to me over a period of years, that I would have volumes to write about their exotic way of life, but in my experience there was very little evidence of it on the surface. It is true that whenever Denys was in Nairobi he used Karen's house as his headquarters; on one occasion he invited me out there to do a portrait of her, an offer which I regret I never took the opportunity of accepting.

Kenyan Characters

It is undeniable that a large number of people were attracted to the country who might be described as characters. Norman Leys, a former official, has compared them in his book to the Elizabethan adventurers such as Drake and Raleigh. Among those who would answer to his description were Denys Finch-Hatton, Lord Delamere, Berkeley Cole and Ewart Grogan to mention only a

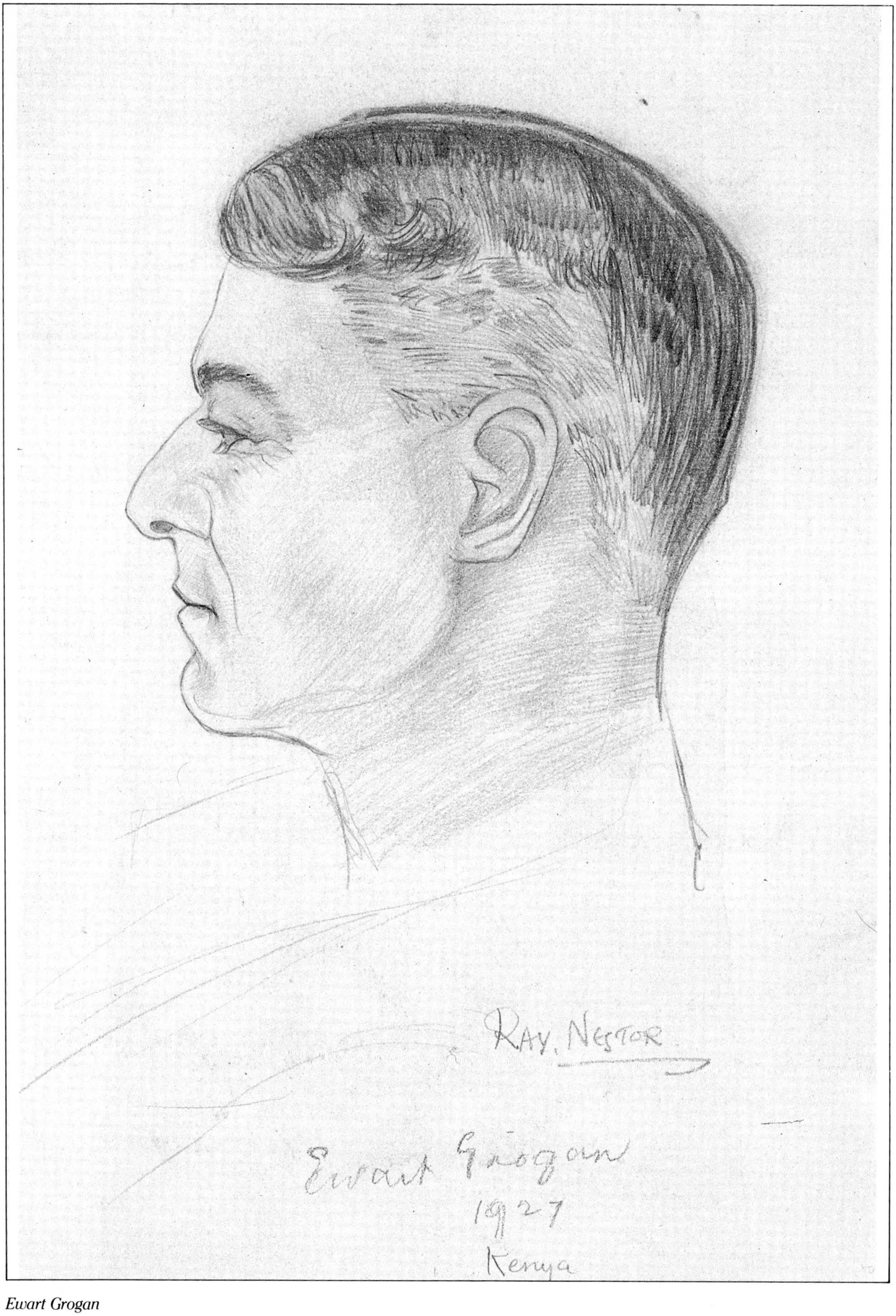

Ewart Grogan

Berkeley Cole

few. The one who impressed me most, perhaps because I had known him all my life, and he was something of a hero to me was my uncle, Jim Corbett, who came to Kenya after the Second World War.

Jim Corbett

Lieut. Colonel Edward James (Jim) Corbett CIE, OBE (1875-1955) was world renowned as a hunter of man-eating tigers and leopards in India. He was noted for his books such as *The Man Eaters of Kumaon; The Man-Eating Leopard of Rudraprayag; Jungle Lore* and *Tree Tops* – his last work which he wrote in 1952. In a letter to me dated 24 March in that same year, he wrote:

'The Mau Mau were giving trouble and I was out with Maggie (his sister) one evening looking for tracks in a ravine, while a polo match was in progress. Everyone in Nyeri and for a hundred miles was at the match, and the one person the Princess asked for was not there. Next morning, while I was shaving, a telephone message came through from the Royal Lodge informing me that the Princess desired my company at Tree Tops. I will tell you the whole story one day, for I know the two of you will be as proud as Maggie and I are that for a whole night I had the honour of being the only one in the world on guard on the person of the Queen.'

It will be remembered that the news of the death of King George VI, was brought to Princess Elizabeth, as she then was, while on a visit to Tree Tops. (It

Lord Delamere, the leader of the white settlers

should be explained that Tree Tops consisted of a platform built into a large fig tree overlooking a salt lick. Rooms were built on the platform, but the accommodation was necessarily very limited.)

This grand old man of 77 was so proud to be on guard, he sat up all night on the top step of the ladder leading to the platform, as he thought, very reasonably, that a leopard could easily climb the steps, and may even have used the platform as an observation post or a place to sleep at night.

He was asked to write up, in the log maintained at Tree Tops, an account of all the animals that had been seen that night and he said. 'I ended my article by saying: "For the first time in the history of the world a young girl climbed into a tree a Princess, and after having what she described as one of the most exciting experiences, she climbed down from the tree next day a Queen".' A copy of the log was later sent to the Queen.

In the last war Jim Corbett trained allied troops for jungle fighting against the Japanese and was given the 'Freedom of Forests' by India for shooting a leopard which killed 125 people.

When he died in Nyeri, Kenya, in his eightieth year, he was extolled in the newspapers of every country, into whose languages his stories had been translated. He had a bookshelf in his room at the Outspan Hotel, which extended right across one wall, filled with these translations.

In the obituary columns of the English papers it was announced that 'Tiger man Jim Corbett dies.' 'All lovers of wild life are the poorer for Jim Corbett's passing.' 'He had an almost uncanny knowledge of the jungle and power to interpret and imitate the noises of beast and bird . . . He insisted that the tiger is never a man-eater by choice and turns to human food only because of incapacity resulting from old age or wounds.'

Lord Delamere

Hugh Cholmondeley, 3rd Baron Delamere, 1870-1931: the most outstanding character in the early days in Kenya was Lord D. – as he was called by everyone. He was the accepted leader of the settler community and his life in Kenya was a history of the colony. To those who are looking for a comprehensive account of Lord Delamere's life and the history of Kenya should read Elspeth Huxley's fine book *White Man's Country, Lord Delamere and the Making of Kenya.*

Lord Delamere arrived in Kenya in 1897, the year the first rails of the Uganda Railway were laid; in the First World War he played an important part in pacifying the Masai, when they rebelled in 1918. They had refused to enlist and after an engagement with the King's African Rifles, when some of them were killed, they got out of hand. It was a dangerous situation and Delamere offered to negotiate. I believe he was a blood brother of the Masai. He met them, accompanied by a few of his own trusted servants, armed only with a revolver. And he succeeded in persuading the Masai to allow their moran warriors to join the KAR.

Lord Delamere was the biggest land owner in Kenya, with 42,000 acres at Soysambu and a grant of 100,000 acres at Njoro. He spent his money lavishly on improvements, such as pipelines to supply water to the dry areas of his land, and by importing pedigree stock.

It must have been a very great disappointment to him to see the fruits of his efforts crumbling to pieces, as they did with the falling land values when he died at the height of the Slump in 1931. He was a great pioneer and the father of white settlement in Kenya, the country he made his home.

I executed two portraits of Lord Delamere, one of which he accepted as a wedding present when he married his second wife, Lady Markham; the second, a pencil portrait which is in Muthaiga Club.

Lt. Colonel Ewart Scott Grogan

Lt. Colonel Ewart Scott Grogan DSO, was perhaps the most Elizabethan type of character.

Grogan was an Irishman, with the gift of the gab. A fine speaker, he was in great demand to give talks on his exploits. I well remember calling at his house, to do a sketch, and found him reading a dictionary; words were a great interest to him. The book by which he will, perhaps be best remembered is entitled *From the Cape to Cairo.* It was an exploit which places him among the foremost explorers of Africa. He wrote it when he was a young man and dedicated it 'To the Memory of the Greatest and most far-seeing of British Imperial Statesmen, the Rt. Hon. Cecil John Rhodes . . .' Rhodes, in his introduction, wrote: 'I must say I envy you, for you have done that which has been for centuries the ambition of every explorer namely, to walk through Africa from South to North. The amusement of the whole thing is that a youth from Cambridge during his vacation should have succeeded in doing that which the ponderous explorers of the world have failed to accomplish. There is a distinct humour in the whole thing. It makes me the more certain that we shall complete the telegraph and railway, for surely I am not going to be beaten by the legs of a Cambridge undergraduate.'

Grogan had many stirring adventures on his journey, shooting as he went. His route was very direct. From the Cape he went to Bulawayo and on to the left of the Victoria Falls, and so to Broken Hill. Then he proceeded through North-Eastern Rhodesia and a long way up to the west of Victoria Nyanza and Kampala in Uganda, which was about half-way. Thence he continued to Kero, the frontier station of the Congo Free State (now Zaire) on the Nile. From here he paddled up the Nile in a canoe to Bohr and on through a channel cut in the mud. In Duika Land he had a skirmish with the natives. Continuing through the swamps, they frequently waded in the water up to their necks, and eventually he contacted Captain Hayes Sadler who gave him a lift in a gun-boat to Khartoum and on to Omdurman where he met Sir Francis Wingate. The remainder of the journey was by railway and steamer to Asswuan and finally to Cairo. It took him over 14 months, and he carried a Union Jack, which is preserved in Groote Schuur, Cape Town, the house built by Rhodes for the Prime Ministers of South Africa.

Denys Finch-Hatton

The Hon. Denys Finch-Hatton was also the type to conform closely to Norman Leys' comparisons to Drake and Raleigh. He was tall and exceptionally strong. At one time he overturned his car into a drain, but lifted it so as to crawl out. As a big-game hunter he took out many important safaris, including that for HRH the Prince of Wales.

Photography was one of his hobbies and he had some exceptional photographs of lions climbing trees. But he was also an intellectual and was often invited to stand for Legislative Council, but refused. Denys's chief hobby was flying. There was a special plot of land on the Nairobi Hill which he wished to apply for, it was Crown Land and he asked me to look at it. The best way was to fly over, so I accompanied him.

He had a Moth Biplane. I had never flown before, and I found it to be a most enthralling experience. The plane was a two-seater, just broad enough to seat a passenger in front and the pilot at the back. You could look over either side and gauge the drop to the ground. We circled around the plot of land in question and over Nairobi and Muthaiga, landing back on the aerodrome. Having landed me, he said he intended to go up again and do a loop. 'Would you like to come?' he asked. 'Of course, I would,' I replied. So up we went again.

I shall never forget this one and only occasion I ever 'looped-the-loop.' It is

commenced at maximum speed with a dive, then a rise and a backward turn upside-down. One is inclined to watch the horizon for balance, when it suddenly disappears and you are looking straight down into the ground. It is most confusing. Before one has time to collect one's bearings, you are back in the straight and the manoeuvre is completed.

I wondered later if that was the first loop he had ever done. He was inclined to take a risk. Lord Delamere mentioned how one day he had laid out a sheet on his farm to practise golf shots. All of a sudden an aeroplane appeared in the sky. They had never seen one above the farm before and they made a hurried exit from the spot as the plane landed. It was Denys and a friend who had lost their way.

"After I had left Africa, Gustav Mohr wrote to me of a strange thing that had happened by Denys's grave, the like of which I have never heard. 'The Masai' he wrote, have reported to the District Commissioner at Ngong, that many times, at sunrise and sunset, they have seen lions on Finch-Hatton's grave in the hills. A lion and a lioness have come there and stood, or lain, on the grave for a long time."

Karen Blixen, Out of Africa

Lake Naivasha

There were a number of fine farms and houses along the shores of Lake Naivasha. One of these belonged to Capt. and Mrs Carnelly, who very kindly at a later date, lent it to my wife and me for a couple of weeks' holiday, while they lived in the house we rented in Muthaiga. Our hosts had designed and built this double-storied Elizabethan-style house themselves and it could hardly have been set in a more beautiful situation, standing, as it did, within sight of both the main lake and the inner lake of Naivasha. There were many fine specimens of the lovely yellow thorn fever tree, the stem of which is of great beauty, chiefly silver, with areas of red, green and yellow. The Carnellys were keen preservers of all types of game, not only on their own land, but also in the lake, where large parties of hippo could be seen at any time. It was a delight to take a chair and sit quietly by the water. The hippo would soon accept the intrusion, and

Denys Finch-Hatton, I knew him very well for the last ten years of his life, we discussed flying together from Kenya to England in his aeroplane

Lake Naivasha

would commence to gambol and play about with each other, accompanied by deep guttural sounds like chuckles of laughter. They could be watched from quite close, certainly not more than 50 yards away, and I was able to make sketches of them partially screened by clumps of papyrus grass. Not only the hippo, but other types of small animals such as dik-dik, would cautiously approach and sniff delicately to reassure themselves that all was well. The only ones that had to be guarded against were the wild pig, which were dangerous if accompanied by their young. The Carnellys had a number of tame crested cranes, and they had the habit of pecking out the putty from the window panes, and admiring themselves in the glass. The cry of the eagle could be heard in the sky; it is the most arresting wild free sound that could be imagined.

Practically all the lakes of Kenya, such as Nakuru Lake and Elementeita, as well as Naivasha, which were such beauty spots and assets to the country, not only on account of the water, but because they provided the homes for vast numbers of birds and beasts, have partially dried up.

The flocks of flamingoes on all these lakes, and particularly Lake Nakuru, were a great attraction not only to the local inhabitants but also to visitors. But they have very largely disappeared. It was a paradise in those early days. There was of course a reason for this drying up, and it had been explained in letters to the press and in complaints to government for many years. But either the remedy was too difficult to enforce or it was not accepted. The cause of the trouble was the denudation of the catchment areas of the vegetation, which nature has provided to control the movement of rainwater and prevent flooding on the one hand, or the drying up of the land on the other. The grass, undergrowth and trees act as a sponge to prevent the excessive flow of heavy rain, or to release such water as the vegetation is in want of over dry periods. Unfortunately, many landowners were confirmed burners, and even if they did not themselves fire the dry grass, they were not interested or concerned to prevent or control the blaze once started. It was contended by them that the fires were started by the natives to provide fresh grazing for their cattle, but this was partly an excuse, as I have had personal experience of landowners setting fire to their dry grass themselves, and when one was asked, why he did it, he said he was trying to tidy up his farm. That the grass cover over earth not only prevents surface erosion, but also the loss of large quantities of the soil, can be proved by a simple experiment. If two receptacles are filled with loose earth, the one without any grass cover, while the other is covered with sods of grass, and water is poured over each, it will be found that the water draining through the receptacle with the loose earth will be dark brown in colour, showing that it contains particles of earth; whereas the one covered with a mat of grass will permit the water to pass through it without any sediment, and will look like clean water. This experiment was demonstrated by Major Ward, who started the Arbour Society in Nairobi, and worked diligently to further its ends, and protect the flora of the country from destruction.

Lakes Nakuru and Elementeita have suffered in the same way, as has Naivasha, as a result of the denudation and destruction of their catchment areas.

The 'Boom' of the 1920s

The forward policy of Sir Edward Grigg, who was Governor of Kenya from 1925-1931, and the extensive building programme in Nairobi, together with the influx of capital brought in, and the enterprise stimulated by the Royal safaris, resulted in a boom throughout the country.

Land values started to rise with the demand for farming produce, and government seized the opportunity of holding an auction of land, including some of the 160 acre A-farms that had not yet been allocated in the Kibigori area.

The Indian community were at the auction in large numbers as they were chiefly farming in this area on account of the hot and humid climate which suited them more than it did the European settlers. But there were also a few Europeans representing important interests in the neighbourhood. It was, in fact, a very well-attended sale, and the conditions of purchase were very easy, being approximately 10 per cent of the purchase price down and the remainder payable over a long or short period, whichever suited the purchaser, at a low rate of interest.

These conditions were very attractive to the Indians, and the plots, which were chiefly 160 acres each, were knocked down at high prices from 35,000 shillings to 60,000 shillings, say an average of £2,000 per farm. This was very surprising indeed, and I congratulated myself on the possession of my 800-odd acres. I argued, as I thought not unreasonably, that these could be considered to be low prices, since this was a young country and bound to go ahead. My farm should be worth at least £15,000. A friend came to me after the sale and offered me £4,000 on behalf of a buyer; a very substantial profit considering that I had paid less than £1,000. But I refused, I would not accept less than £7 per acre, say £5,500, and so after a certain amount of bickering the sale fell through. I was quite happy. But not for long.

The demand, for no obvious reason, started to hang fire. And as years passed I found that there was less and less interest in my Kibigori land. An Indian bought two of my five A-farms at £2 per acre in 1929; I kept the remaining three farms, in one unit, still quite sure that the prices would go up.

However, the sale of my two farms in 1929 rewarded me in a far better way than the mere possession of the money, because it helped me to meet the

young lady to whom I got married. I used part of the proceeds to go on a cruise and we were both on the same boat voyaging to Singapore on 'a slow boat to China'. It was what may be decribed as a 'whirlwind' courtship, since we knew each other for less than a month; but it proved to be a great success, and the best investment I ever made, with a quick profit.

Lake Elmenteita, where flamingoes gathered in huge numbers

The Building Scheme

In 1930 Government also introduced what was known as the Building Scheme, with the object of encouraging officials to build their own houses, since there was a shortage of quarters available which were part of a civil servant's emoluments, or an allowance in lieu. There were excellent sites on the Crown Land situated on Nairobi Hill, the most desirable residential quarter.

My wife and I applied for permission to join the scheme, and obtained a three-acre plot on a bluff with a southern aspect overlooking a plain extending for hundreds of miles with a distant view of Mount Kilimanjaro on the Tanganyika border over a hundred miles away 'as the crow flies'. It was at the back of, and within a quarter of a mile of Nairobi Club. The ground in front of the house dropped steeply to a small river course at its base, and a vast plain extended for hundreds of miles as far as the eye could see, past a well known landmark known as 'lone tree', the recognised haunt of a pride of lions. At all times of the day, but particularly in the early mornings and evenings, the view was breathtaking. There were no houses in sight and the rolling clouds cast their

Rhino with Kilimanjaro in the background

shadows on the brown grass and trees, very much in the same way as clouds over a long sea view. The varying shades and textures of the irregularly shaped shadows on this vast palette assumed all sorts of lovely colours, chiefly pale pinks or violets and russets. It was a delight to us.

And my wife Dorothy, who was a keen gardener, decided to plant a garden worthy of our property. Day after day she could be seen under a large sunhat, accompanied by two 'shamba boys', busily planting out our rose garden, and large numbers of fig tree branches bought from the forest department which we were assured would grow easily into trees. These were certainly needed badly to beautify our plot, which was quite bare of trees, except for a single struggling 'mattundu' which we were just in time to save from the ministrations of our builders who considered it to be an obstruction. Every weekend, I drove the car round to find Kikuyu grass to plant up our plot, which was very largely rock outcrop.

One thing for which we had not contended was the game. The zebra and kongori soon discovered our nice new succulent flower beds, and arrived in droves every night. We were awakened regularly with the stamping of hoofs outside our bedroom windows, and it was easy to lean out and smack the zebra with a stick across the bottom. They were, or rather they acted practically as household pets. Eventually I decided the only thing to do was to fence in the three acres, rather an unexpected expense. A contractor erected a four-strand barbed wire fence, which was regularly knocked down in parts where the herd decided to take a short-cut out, on those occasions when they were suddenly frightened, probably by our dogs starting to bark.

One night when the fence was first erected, but the gate had not been affixed, we decided to go to the theatre. And it was almost laughable and comical to find that we had to stop the car in our own drive, while a herd of at least 30 zebra nonchalantly walked in twos and threes straight into the glare of our headlights to eat our flowers. It was an unforgettable sight to see the brilliant dancing eyes of our visitors as they bobbed their heads up and down. And we had to accept their presence or risk our newly-restored fence from being smashed down once again.

Shortly after we had built our house, the country suffered one of its worst locust invasions. It was quite an alarming sight to watch the approach of the swarm, as it did from a northernly direction, spreading right across the sky. A thin dark line was first observed 30 miles long on the horizon, which gradually broadened and deepened in colour as it came nearer. It was a dark purple or red like a dense rain cloud, and it continued to darken the sky till the sun was almost blotted out. Presently the vanguard arrived flying in all directions, so that they were difficult to dodge, and it was advisable to take cover to avoid being hit in the face. The birds attacked at first and gorged themselves until they were overcome. When the alarm was first given we lit fires in the hope that the smoke would drive them away, or at any rate discourage them from settling on our land, but it was useless. They arrived in their millions and the weight of their numbers broke branches off the trees and shrubs where they settled. They ate every bit of greenery much more thoroughly than a herd of goats or sheep. Even the washing hanging out on the lines had to be hurriedly brought in or they would eat it. The infestation was so heavy that it even stopped the traffic; the roads were made too slippery as the bodies were crushed beneath the wheels of cars.

For days the locusts covered every available surface and the authorities were powerless to deal with the situation. Finally, the swarms from the roads were swept into the storm water drains, or other drains were dug alongside and the locusts were brushed into them and poisoned with an arsenical spray. Unfortunately the poison also had the effect of killing much of the bird life. These locusts are known as desert locusts and can only breed on barren ground. It was curious that one could actually hear a swarm of locusts eating the grass.

Locust invasions were by no means recent events. An old Kenya settler said he first saw them in 1895, and again in 1897, when they were followed by rinderpest owing to the cattle not having enough grazing.

The Slump

In Kenya the mid-1920s had been a period of prosperity, but towards the end of Sir Edward Grigg's term as governor, the greatest slump the world had ever known broke in America, and he was severely criticised for his extravagance over the extensive building programme he had begun but, fortunately for Kenya, it had to be completed as orders could not be cancelled.

This was the first indication of trouble that was to come, but generally we viewed the situation with complacency, thinking that a catastrophe in America was too far away to effect us.

On every side there was evidence of prosperity. We, ourselves, enjoyed a high

New Nairobi market early 1930s

standard of living with our house and car, and we were in a position to entertain our friends lavishly at dinner with three or four courses and the appropriate wines and spirits convention demanded. Also, we had numbers of servants to minister to our wants. It seemed incredible that anything could touch us. We were delighted with our house and possessions, and with the results of the hard work we put in to beautify and improve our property. But fate decreed that we were to enjoy it for only one year.

Gradually warnings appeared in Kenya that the economic situation was worsening. Many officials in Kenya were retrenched in 1931 and 1932. I had just completed my first tour of service since my marriage, and was due for 'home' leave in England. Also I had just qualified for pension after 20 years' service in 1932. I was therefore apprehensive of my chances of retrenchment.

The head of my department asked me if I would like to be retired. I told him it would be a calamity for me with my commitments. I had, fortunately, just completed the payments for my De Soto car, but the instalments for the payment of my house and land were in the early stages. I had also to carry on with the expenses of my coffee farm at Kipkarren which was a heavy liability.

But I said that I was aware that I was perhaps due for retirement in preference to others more junior than myself who had not qualified for pension. I would be grateful, however, if I might be informed whether or not I was likely to be retrenched before I left Kenya, in order that I might make the necessary arrangements. I was informed that my name was not on the list for retrenchment. Consequently, I let my house in Nairobi for only six months, as I would require it on my return to Kenya from leave.

Gibraltar sketched from on-board ship

And so passages were booked to England for my wife and myself on the S.S. *Llanstephan Castle,* a 11,293 ton boat, on the 12 June 1932, the height of the world slump, and we landed in London on 4 July. We got an excellent double room in a Lancaster Gate hotel, overlooking Hyde Park, for only six guineas a week full-board for the two of us. In spite of the assurance, given me in Kenya, that I would not be retrenched, I was worried about it, and therefore asked the Colonial Office if I might return early and spend two months of my leave in Kenya. This permission was granted, and we felt justified in buying clothing, linen and other articles we needed.

By a stroke of bad luck, my wartime disability broke out again, and I was admitted into Queen Mary's Military Hospital at Roehampton, where I had to undergo a number of operations and remained there for nearly six months. It was a chamber of horrors in the corrugated iron officers' ward, where some of the patients were frightfully mutilated and had been there for years. Shortly after I entered hospital at Roehampton, I received a letter from Kenya to say I was retrenched.

As a concession the Colonial Office allowed me full pay while in hospital and gave us first-class fares to return to Kenya.

Confronted as I was with the prospect of living on half my salary, I totted up my 'irreducible' expenses, and decided that it could not be done. There were taxes for the car, the gun, the dogs; education and poll tax and wireless license; rents for the farms and the house plot in Nairobi; subscriptions to the clubs; instalments for the payment of the house; repayment of the loan to the Land Bank. And we still had to pay our servants, run our car and provide ourselves with food and clothing.

It appeared to be formidable, but it is surprising how easy things are if they have to be done. Our first decision was whether to try and keep the house or the farm. There was no sale for the farm, so we had to part with the house. Fortunately, the government agreed to accept the house instead of the money

Forest on our farm.

outstanding. The other commitments happened to be unimportant or easily solved.

Some kind friends on a coffee farm at Kabete, three miles from Nairobi offered us their manager's cottage, as they had had to dispense with his services owing to the slump. It is ironical that the coffee crop from this farm, when prices recovered, was sold for an average of £500 a ton and they marketed no less than 70 tons. It was a great advantage for me to be on an established coffee farm, as it gave me an opportunity of learning, at first hand, how to manage such an estate as we intended to go to Kipkarren and run our coffee farm ourselves.

And so we made our preparations. I was aware that my manager's old wattle and daub thatched house was no longer habitable, as it was now used as a store for the farm implements, but we were lucky to be lent an old stone house by a friend. It had been unoccupied for three or four years, and was in a very dilapidated condition, and our friend was only too pleased to allow us to live in it, provided we made whatever improvements and renovations necessary.

One of our neighbours cleaned it up for us and cut a rough path from the main road through the bush, before our arrival. Others arrranged to supply us with provisions such as vegetables and milk, which we would at first be unable to provide for ourselves. With the slump on we were all in the same boat and the farmers were very hard-hit. It is curious how 'one touch of nature', or a slump 'makes the whole world kin'. Many farms had been abandoned, so as new arrivals we were made very welcome.

We hired a railway truck from Nairobi to Eldoret and packed all our furniture into it. We, ourselves, travelled up by road in my box body De Soto car, accompanied by a Kikuyu servant and our dog John, a brindle bull terrier.

We were now launched on a new stage of our existence.

Life at Kipkarren

At Kipkarren, also, there was ample evidence of the serious depression in the farming community, where the prices reached a record low. Mealies or Indian corn was only 3/6 a bag, and 'posho', the staple food made from it for the African natives was 5 shillings a bag.

Many of the 160-acre, Soldier Settlement A-farms, were abandoned, and the owners were either repatriated or had left their farms to try their luck in the goldfields at Kakamega, where gold had recently been discovered about 30 miles from my farm. Within a couple of years over £200,000 of gold was produced, and many companies were formed – some of a very dubious nature.

This was a well-watered area and most of the prospecting was alluvial; faint traces of gold were even panned in my own stream. But of course the chief basis of gold mining is from reefs, and my neighbour was one of those who was lucky to strike a rich vein, which he quickly sold for the large sum of £50,000. He was the only one, I knew of, to make a success of it, but at least one other did well by selling worthless shares.

Life at Kipkarren was rough, but we found it interesting in contrast to our previous existence. Our first job was to clean up the house, lent to us at Kipkarren, which was infested with rats and snakes. The noise made by the rats kept us awake, and one night I tried to locate the spot in the floor where they were gnawing. I got out of bed and bent down to listen, and there was a snake near my bare feet. It was amusing to see the way he attempted to camouflage himself by lying along the junction of two planks of wood. I realised that he was after the rats, so I simply picked him up on a stick and threw him out of the front door.

Another time our house boy lifted a chop box, and carried it into the next room, with a look on his face as though he was going to be sick. He had seen a snake coiled below the box as he lifted it, but such was his respect for property that he did not drop the box. But by the time I got there the snake had disappeared. It was very unaccountable, as it could not have escaped through the door or window. We found, however, that all the skirtings along the floor were loose, and when they were removed large numbers of rat and snake holes were disclosed. A few shovels of cement soon remedied the trouble.

The place had so largely reverted to jungle that the animal and insect life resented our occupation. Baboons, that had been accustomed to raid the guava trees, still arrived in troops. One big baboon on my approach, nonchalantly climbed down and walked away slowly, looking over his shoulder with a disdainful air; so that my houseboy remarked: 'Sawa, Sawa Bwana', just like a Bwana (master). There were plenty of buck and leopards about. We had taken our dog John with us, and he appreciated or recognised that this was a wild country unlike Nairobi, so when I opened the door for him to take a run at night before going to bed, he would emerge making all the noise he was capable of,

Nandi Elmoran

barking and howling 'like a lion', and for all I know he might have frightened the leopards and other prowlers away.

One morning, while we were about our household duties, we heard a great blowing of horns, and a bugle playing military calls very well indeed. Presently, large numbers of young Nandi 'elmoran' or warriors appeared with swords, spears and their shields painted in bold designs. Their hair was carefully dressed with pigtails plastered with red mud.

We were a little apprehensive at first, but soon realised that they were out to give us a treat, on the way to a leopard hunt. The leopard had killed some goats and was located in a clump of dense forest about a mile away, down on a river bank. So I decided to take my .303 rifle and join the party, where some of the elders had gathered on a little hillock with a good view of the proceedings. I was made welcome and accepted as an equal. The Kenya natives are never diffident like the Indians, if they know you and meet you in the street some months later, they are just as likely to greet you as an old friend, and hold out their hand to shake.

While we waited on the hillock, parties of moran would arrive at intervals with enormous dramatic affect. Twenty or more at a time would swoop down on us 'like a wolf on the fold', waving their spears, swords and shields, and with one accord they would drive their spears into the ground and sit down in silence. They were a fine sight with their heads painted with red and yellow ochre. Presently other parties would arrive, all in the same manner, till there must have been well over a hundred of them.

While we waited, some of the young bloods became restive, and doubtless they had been having a beer drink. One young fellow, whether to impress me or not, I was not sure, gave a spirited display, circling round and round waving his spear and making a pass at the other braves, who rested on their haunches in silence.

A master of ceremonies eventually decided the time had arrived to start the hunt. So a party of young men went into the forest to drive the leopard out, while the killers made a phalanx sinking on one knee with their shields in front of them and their spears at the ready. All this time they made as much noise as they could to frighten the animal, blowing their horns, beating drums and shouting. There was so much confusion, the leopard, if one had been there, would surely have escaped. But I rather thought the whole performance was largely an excuse for a party. This continued for so long, and as it looked like rain, I decided it was time for lunch.

Late in the afternoon, at least five hours after the start, my headman called in to tell me it was over; a big leopard had been killed and one toto, while a second toto had escaped.

The next day they arrived at the house with the skin, which they offered to sell to me for ten shillings. But it was so badly mutilated with holes, there was not sufficient skin to make a handbag. Besides which, I did not wish to encourage the destruction of the leopards, which were so useful in keeping down the numbers of the baboons. Indeed the baboons were far more to be feared, and I was careful to go out for walks over the hills, where they were, armed with a gun. They were not unlikely to attack John, our dog, and would bark at him angrily whenever they caught sight of him.

Head of Nandi Elmoran

There were troops of colobus monkeys in the trees, and John frightened a baby who could not move, so I picked it up and took it home as its mother had run away. It must have had too much of a shock, as it did not live through the night.

Another time, while walking through the forest I saw a little dik-dik caught in a trap, probably laid by the garden 'shamba' boy. I picked it up and held it while I tried to loosen the noose. It made no attempt to struggle and appeared to be resigned to its fate. All the time it watched me with the most beautiful liquid eyes imaginable, and when at last I got it free and placed it on the ground, it stood quite still near my feet, until I bent down to see if it was all right, when it awakened to the fact that it had no more to fear and dashed off through the undergrowth.

One day, the Paramount Chief of the Nandi came in to see me, this was Arap Katono, who had a big farm with tractors of his own to plough up his land. He deplored the fact that his new status and prosperity still had its drawback. 'You

Young Nandi girl, the Nandi were our immediate neighbours

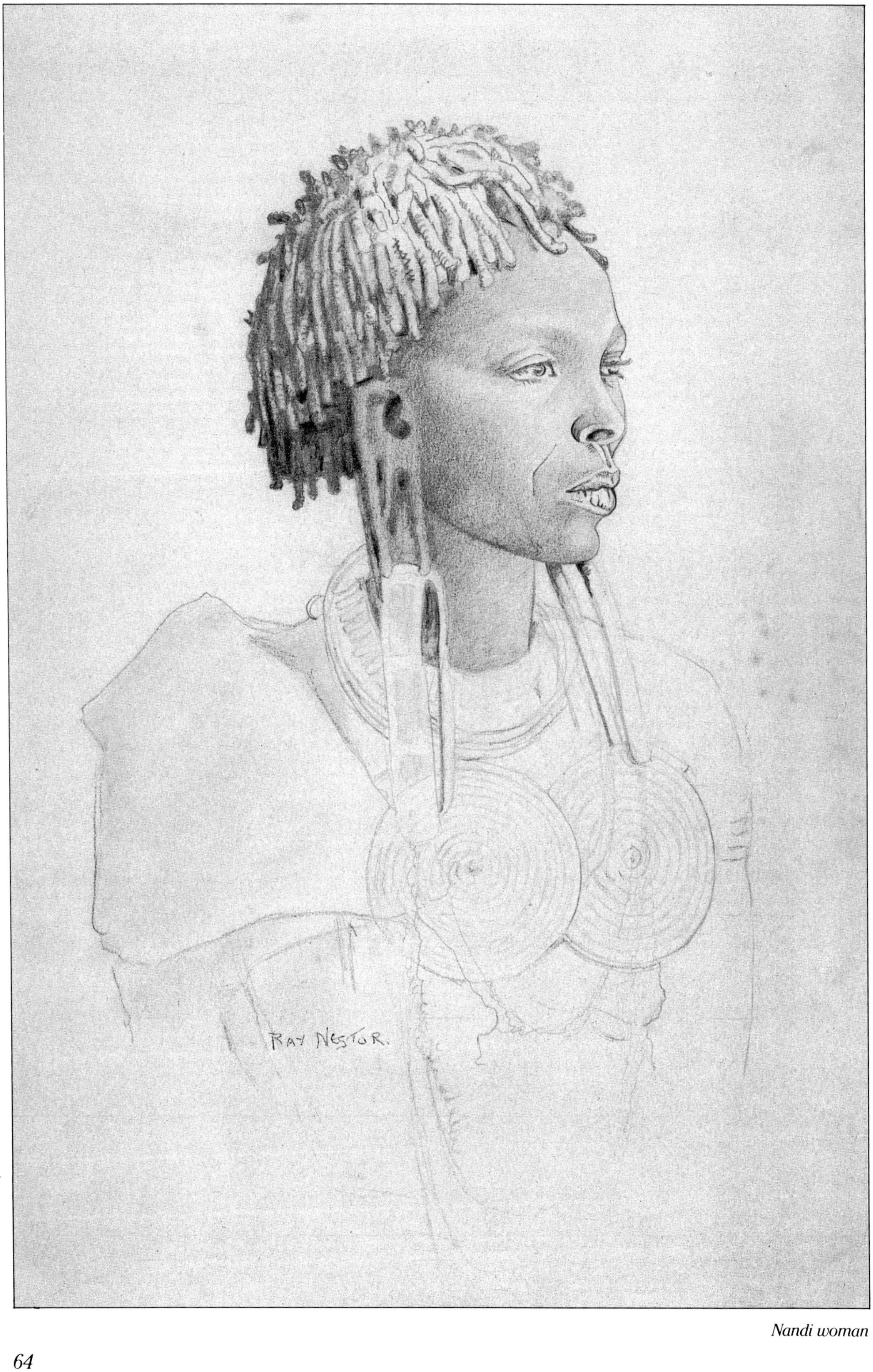

Nandi woman

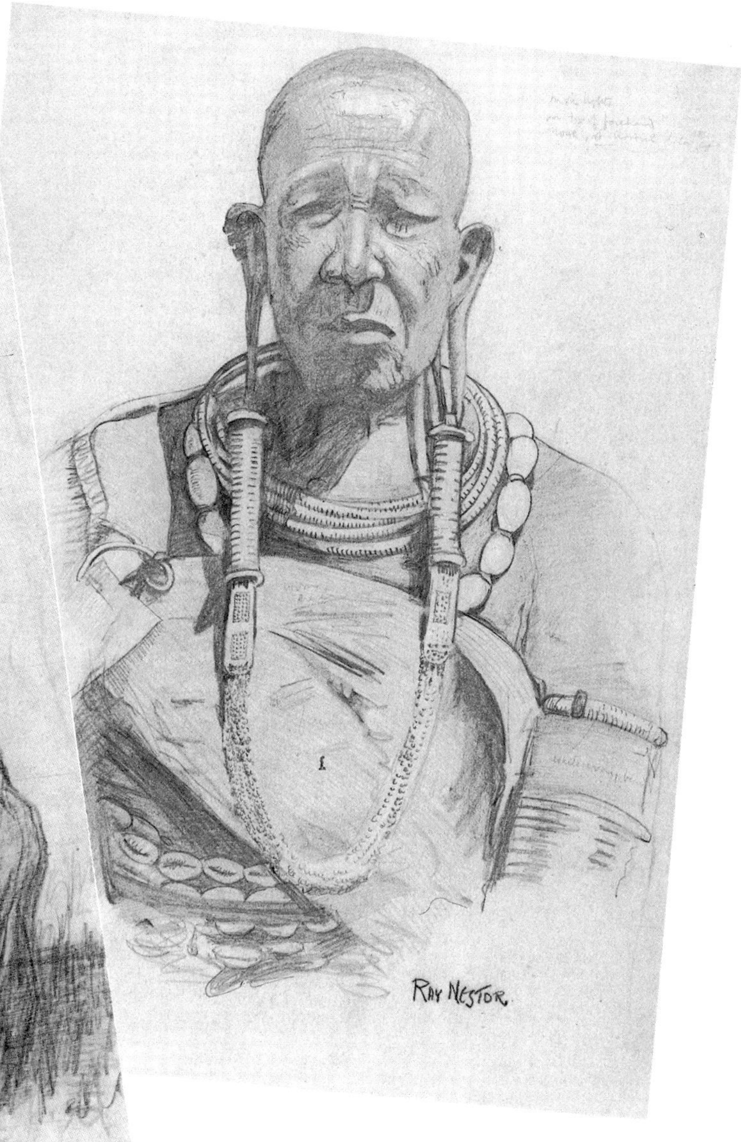

An old Nandi woman the natives all called Mama

An old man who always asked my permission to graze his cattle on government land, which he could not understand I had no right to give

see,' he said, 'I have to keep on buying new pairs of boots, as my feet are now too soft to walk barefooted, yet my father had no need for even a single pair of boots all his life.'

Then again we had a visit from a mad old Nandi woman, who refused to leave and insisted on hanging about the boys' quarters. We discovered her first one afternoon when we were taking a rest and John, our dog, barked. She was just off our verandah, and when I came out she ran a short distance away, giggling and waving her arms. She was an old woman with a withered and lined face, but tall and thin. She was dressed in the usual native apron made of hides which covered her legs, and round her waist wore a broad belt of about eight inches, covered in cowrie shells. Above the waist she was naked, and her long thin arms and shrivelled hanging breasts were very noticeable. When I first ordered her away, she actually did leave before long. But the servants told us that she

Our indigenous forest

had been hanging around for some days, and they had to remain on guard, when we went to Eldoret to do our weekly shopping, because they were afraid she might do some damage. They told me she was not a 'maginga' or simple, but described her state as 'zimo' in Swahili 'mad'. She was known to have lived on this shamba or farm for some years, back to the time when it was occupied by an old settler who was called 'bwana maginga', and that she had then set alight to his cattle boma. They said that people like her always set alight to things, and they were very careful, while she was about, to keep their huts shut, so that she should not take a piece of firewood and fire the hut.

They also told me that she took a great interest in our car which we kept in an open shed, saying she would buy one for 100 shillings. (That reminded me that our neighbour had his car burnt one day and no explanation was ever found for it). So the second time I caught her hanging about near the house, I tried to frighten her off. But she refused to be frightened, and would only run around giggling and making a hissing noise, though I never heard her speak a word. She was very active for such an apparently old woman, and would do a curious solo dance, bending and straightening the body and jumping in the air, waving her arms and hissing. I got her some distance away from the house, and we went for a walk but on our return at dusk, there she was again. So I got a stick and approached her threateningly, but she was clearly not a bit afraid and knew that my gesture was all a pretence, and indicated that she was prepared to fight as she carried a couple of heavy sticks herself, and one of these she

The view from our house on the farm at Kipkarren, thorn trees and tame buck

suddenly threw at me. I just had time to duck as it whistled past my head. She certainly was a problem, and I thought discretion was the better part of valour, even Johnny appeared to be afraid of her. However, as night was falling, she made up her mind and went off on her own accord, but I thought it advisable to see that the doors were locked when we went to sleep.

But that was not the last we heard of her, because she transferred her attentions to our thatched farm house, which I kept as a store for my ploughs and implements. Nabulo, my headman, told me he was unable to supervise the labour as he had to stand guard, as he was afraid of the old lady with the 'zimu'. I, therefore, decided to try and put a stop to this business, and went by car to the nearest telephone at our branch post office, over seven miles away, to ring up the police station, a distance of 15 miles further on. We were, indeed, very much cut off and isolated. The police station was manned by a single white policeman, with four or five askaris, to supervise a couple of hundred square miles of territory. He was therefore, as I expected, out, and I had to leave a message with one of the askaris. I also wrote a letter explaining the situation, and reminding him of two recent burnings when many acres of coffee trees had been destroyed, and I referred him to the police case in which two of my own working oxen had been stolen by the Nandi, and slaughtered by them; but although the culprits were discovered and fined, I got no compensation. But the policeman was busy and could not attend to my complaint.

A few days later I had to go to a farmers' meeting some 20 miles away, and when I returned about 4 o'clock in the afternoon, my wife met me with the bad news that 25 acres of coffee trees, nearly half my total acreage, had been burnt out during the morning, as well as over 50 acres of open land.

The Grass Fire Ordinance

After the burning of my coffee bushes I commenced my campaign against 'Grass Fires'. Every year at Kipkarren, just before the rainy season, the whole countryside was enveloped in smoke, sometimes for months on end. The burning of the grass and vegetal cover is the most important and pressing problem in Kenya. My campaign was the one major contribution which I have made to the land of Kenya in return for the happiness and health it has given me, and that of which I am most proud. In Nairobi we formed the Arbour Society which was started by Major Ward who was most enthusiastic and helpful. We succeeded, in the end, in forcing Government to bring in the 'Grass Fire Ordinance'.

It happened in this way: I continued to draw attention to, and to complain of, the burning at our Farmers' Meetings, until one of the members, more as a joke than anything else, said, 'Why don't you stop it?' I accepted their challenge and as I realised the only way to obtain the ear of Government was to submit it under the auspices of a Farmers' Association. Individual appeals such as writing letters to the newpapers made no impression, although this method paved the way by forming public opinion. And I was grateful to Mr Kinear, the Editor of the *East African Standard*, for his fine leading articles on the subject.

When given permission to use the authority of the Kipkarren Farmers' Association, I immediately circularised all the other Farmers' Assocations, and any other important bodies such as the Horticultural and Agricultural Societies, even the East African Women's League, and asked for their help. I also wrote to the Agricultural Departments of the Crown Colonies and Dominions, including South Africa, asking them what methods they used to combat this serious problem, stressing the destruction of humus, the world's most valuable asset. The response was most gratifying.

These replies I summarised and submitted to the Government, with the help of the Editor of the *East African Standard*. In addition I wrote to Sir Edward Grigg, the former Governor of Kenya, and through him succeeded in having the situation submitted to the highest authority, the Home Government.

There was opposition to the measure in the Kenya Legislative Council, chiefly on account of the difficulty of enforcing it. However, the Grass Fire Ordinance was finally passed. It provided the penalties against unlawful burning, and defined the obligations of all citizens to assist in extinguishing fires.

At a Farmers' Association meeting, I reported the Grass Fire Ordinance as a 'fait accompli'. It was amusing to see with what bitter opposition it was received by some. Although the campaign had been carried through with their authority, if not entirely with their unanimous approval. One or two said, 'I will burn my land if I like' and one farmer who had been a Director of Agriculture, produced a learned argument to prove that burning was beneficial to the land, on account of the potash it contributed to the soil. This statement was submitted to the Agricultural Department in Kenya, who very wisely supported the contention that burning was, in fact, very bad for the soil, and they produced a pamphlet to prove this.

As an example of the mentality towards the subject of burning, my wife and I while out for a walk on the road passing through our neighbour's farm, saw smoke issuing from a clump of trees and the grass was alight. With great difficulty we beat it out, and when I saw my neighbour the following day I told him how I had saved his farm from burning. But he laughed, 'Oh! that's all right,' he said, 'I fired it myself, I want to tidy up my land'. And he burnt it next day without any attempt at control. It might have travelled for miles before it reached a natural barrier, for all he cared.

It is generally contended that fires are started by the natives, and this is probably true as they are habitual burners for the purpose of providing grazing for their cattle. Another reason for the burning of the grass cover by the natives is in order that buck and other small animals may be more visible, and can consequently be hunted more easily with packs of dogs.

But there is no doubt that the pleasure of seeing a good blaze is ingrained in many people, both black and white. On the road to Eldoret from our farm, we always passed through a fine area of indigenous forest where some employees of the District Council were stationed in their huts. Each time I passed in the car, over a period of months, I saw a native burning the forest. As a matter of interest I stopped one day to ask him what was the object of it, and whether it was being done under instruction by the Council. 'No,' he said, 'I want to stop the hawks and other birds that live in these trees from attacking my chickens.'

The Grass Fire Ordinance was an excellent piece of legislation; it defined the closed season for burning, when it did most harm, but permitted burning of the limited areas, and it made it compulsory for members of the public to help extinguish fires if called upon to do so, with penalties for refusal.

It is easier to introduce legislation than to enforce the measure. However, it had the effect of drawing the attention of the public to the menace and explaining the extent of the damage to the humus and fertility of the soil.

The grass fire on my farm destroyed up to 20 acres of coffee, as I have said, but part of the remaining 40 acres was in fair condition, except for serious gully erosion between the rows of coffee bushes, where my inexperienced manager had plowed directly downhill instead of along the contours. The result was that the heavy rains had washed deep furrows between the rows, even to exposing the roots of some of the trees. Coffee is planted in rows 9 feet apart with 9 feet between each row.

Nobody appeared to know about erosion; I had been advised by the Agricultural department that the first priority was to keep the coffee clean of weeds, and this advice I had passed on to my manager who cleaned the area to such an extent that the surface of the ground, deprived of its cover of protection from the hot sun, had baked to the consistency of a road.

A neighbour, who had been director of Agriculture in Zanzibar advised digging even deeper holes to allow the water to seep through the soil, which was bad advice. Eventually, I discovered the best measure, which was to thatch along the contours with the long grass tied into bundles. Fortunately, there was a plentiful supply of grass available on the farm.

The Agricultural Officer on his next tour of inspection was pleased with the improvement of the coffee plantation and I was rewarded with a fine flowering with a fair crop of coffee.

But that was the last crop of coffee I got from the farm as it was now 1939, just before the start of the Second World War.

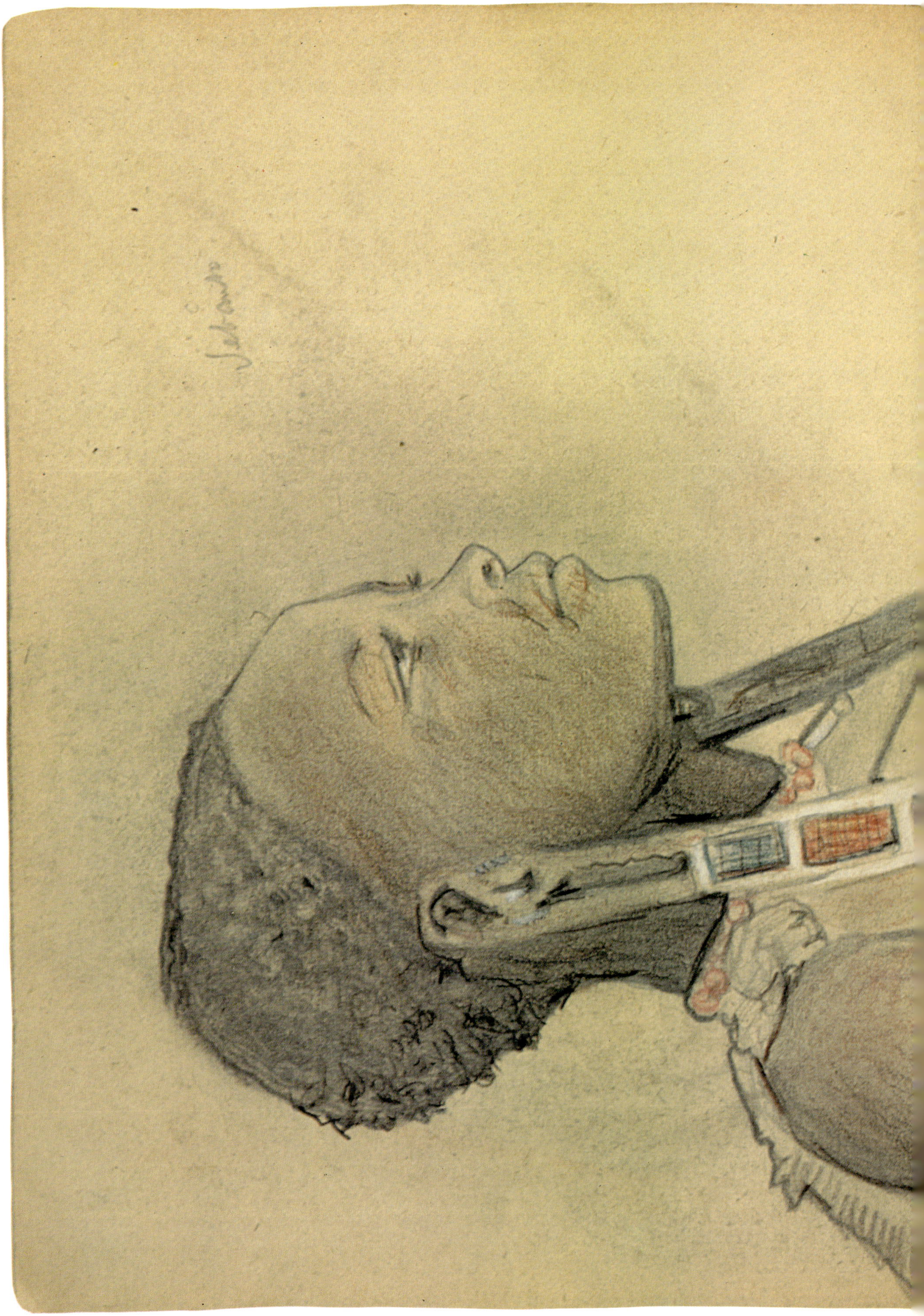

Our gardener's wife who frequently ran away

World War II

On September 1939, we in Kenya received news of the outbreak of World War II. For some months we had been hearing disturbing accounts of Hitler's attacks against Austria and Czechoslovakia, and this final invasion of the Polish Corridor gave England, in view of her recent Polish treaty, no alternative but to declare war against Germany.

The news was therefore not unexpected, but there appeared to be no immediate cause for alarm. Had we not been informed about France's Maginot Line which was considered to be an impregnable barrier to the German advance? And the massing of Allied troops, including the British Expeditionary Force, in Northern France was most reassuring. Nevertheless we all enthusiastically made preparations to join up.

The price of coffee, which I had been growing for over 15 years, was down to rock bottom. When I started farming in about 1922 it was £100 a ton; in 1939 my agents were unable to sell it for more than £39 a ton; at one time, after 1945 a pocket, or a few bags of coffee reached £1,000 a ton.

I had a small loan from the Land Bank of which a debt of £300 was outstanding. Small as it was, I could not pay it off. I was, in fact, not even paying running expenses, and only continued farming in the hopes of better times.

With the news of the declaration of war, there was a rush of disillusioned farmers from the land to join up – including myself. Ironically, those who did not, or could not join up, were lucky, as the prices of all produce soared during and after the war, owing to the drop in production and the heavy extra demand.

However, I was glad to offload my debt to the Land Bank by handing over my 160-acre farm, together with 30-40 acres of standing coffee; and the outbuildings, such as they were, for the £300 outstanding; and for good measure I included all the farm implements, plows, harrows, coffee trays, pulpers, and a considerable amount of oddments such as barrows, pangas and other small items. In any case, they were useless to me, and there was no sale for them then.

And so I made preparations for my departure. I was lucky to have an old friend, 'Dicker' Dickenson, who was head of Intelligence at Force Headquarters, Nairobi. To him I wrote, and heard that he could offer me a vacancy on his staff, which my experience as a surveyor with knowledge of the topography of the country, qualified me to fill.

There were four of us in the office at Force Headquarters, and in the field there were a large number of others who had experience in the past as white hunters and could therefore be relied upon for detailed information about the most remote parts of the country. Major Dickenson, our OC, had himself been a big game hunter before the war and had taken out safaris.

Unfortunately, my First World War disability started up after six months and I had to resign from the Intelligence Department and go to the coast. We rented a bungalow at Nyali, on the mainland across the pontoon bridge from Mombasa.

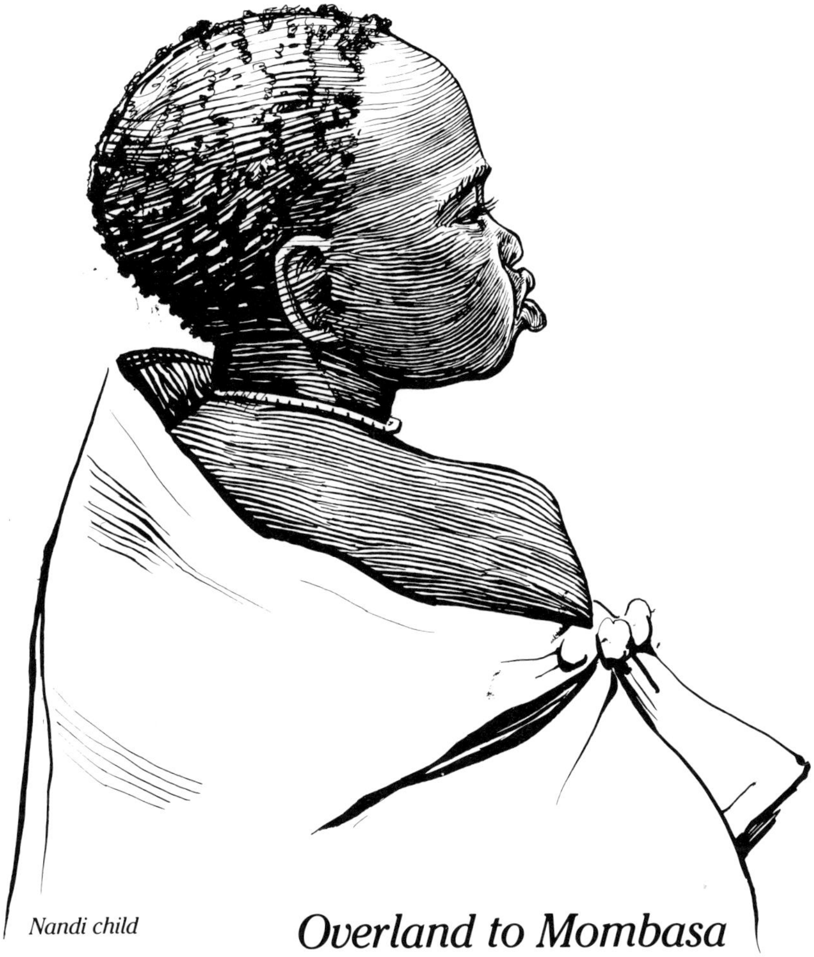

Nandi child

Overland to Mombasa

The journey down from Nairobi to Mombasa was made by car. The distance is about 350 miles, so it meant stopping one night *en route*. We planned to put up at the rest house at Longido on the boundary between Kenya and Tanganyika.

I had a detailed road map, bought some years before, which recommended this rest house. So we travelled along comfortably, taking our time, and arrived at Longido about six o'clock in the evening. To our consternation, we discovered that the rest house had long since ceased to exist. Of course, I should have verified the information before we started, but I didn't. The problem was then whether to return to a hotel we had passed a long way back or continue on to Moshi in Tanganyika where there were many good hotels.

We were advised that it was an easy run, particularly if we took a short cut, and so we set off. About 10 miles on we came to a vast plain which was covered with deep loose dust, which blew up through the chassis, and the road commenced to branch off in all directions. There was no indication which to choose. It was too late to turn back so we decided to take a chance. After travelling some distance, we discovered that the roads joined, and crossed each other, and it was in fact one road about a quarter-of-a-mile broad. it was obvious that previous vehicles had searched around in the hopes of finding a harder road surface without success.

In the course of time, we arrived at the lowest part of the plain where the road ran straight into what looked like a lake, a hundred yards wide. In this sheet of water we could see tall weeds growing, and wildfowl, disturbed by our arrival, rose into the air complaining. It looked so broad, I was worried, and explored up and down the river to see if there was a more suitable crossing, but fortunately, I was not satisfied, so I returned to the car.

The little hut in which we stayed during our enchanting holiday at Bamburi Holiday camp

As there was nothing for it, we had to take a chance telling ourselves that from the look of things other cars must have crossed. It must be a ford. But it was now getting dark and we prayed that we would not be stopped in the middle, or perhaps sink with all aboard.

Fortunately, we crossed safely, and we travelled along the unfamiliar road till we arrived at Moshi, in time for dinner at the 'Lion's Club' Hotel. We told the proprietress of our adventures and fears. She said many people had been in trouble there. Only the previous week, an elderly European had been brought to her hotel in a state of collapse, and had been very ill. He, unfortunately, had made the mistake of deciding to take what he thought was a better crossing, and had nearly drowned in his car. But for the timely arrival of a farmer in the neighbourhood, out shooting wild duck, who rescued him, he would probably have died.

The following day we continued our journey to Mombasa past magnificent views of Mount Kilimanjaro, the highest mountain in Africa. Here were large herds of giraffe, zebra and all kinds of buck to be seen grazing by the roadside.

Mombasa

At Mombasa Club, we got a room with a view overlooking the sea and Fort Jesus. The fort was built by the Portuguese in 1498, where they were besieged by the Arabs for some years, and were finally slaughtered just before the arrival of their fleet which had come to relieve them.

Mombasa, like Zanzibar, was one of the most interesting towns on the East Coast of Africa. Near the Club, is Vasco da Gama Street, so frequently

Arab dhow in full sail at Mombasa

illustrated in photographs and water colours. There is a picture to be seen at every turn. On either side of the street are gaily-coloured houses with magnificent brass-studded Arab doors, and overhanging trellised verandahs. And at the turn is the white Arab Prayer Tower. A feature of many of these streets, are the coloured towels and garments suspended from poles protruding at odd angles from the rafters and verandahs.

Vasco da Gama 'Street, Mombasa

From the scenic point of view the coast itself is most attractive. The streets, bazaars and coast line provide many rewarding subjects for the artist or photographer. The squalid narrow passages in the bazaar, dark and sometimes very dirty, have a mysterious air; but here may be found fine amber necklaces or chased silver bangles to delight the heart of any young woman. Even the collector may discover rare pieces of pottery or porcelain dumped in a corner, covered in dust. The most prized of all, but now rarely to be seen is the brass-studded Lamu Chest. In the old harbour at certain times of the year may be seen dozens of picturesque Arabian dhows at anchor, they arrive from the East with all sorts of strange cargoes.

For the artist and photographer there is one subject to be avoided, and that is the Swahili women. Indeed any attempt to portray them may lead to trouble. These people are Mohammedans and their religion prohibits the representation of the human form. Even in the design of a Persian carpet the human form is rarely seen, though animals are often depicted. But the inclusion of a figure of a woman in a picture, dressed in her long black garment, which covers her from head to foot, with only a narrow slit to show the eyes, provides just that atmosphere of the East so hard to obtain.

The headquarters of the Royal Navy was stationed in Mombasa, and I had gratifying success with the sale of my pictures to the officers and many of the ratings and WRENS. So much so, that I decided to hold a one-man show and the manager of the Manor Hotel very kindly gave me permission to have my exhibition in one of the main rooms. My wife and I, with the help of my Wakamba servant, hung the pictures and we placed a few posters around to advertise the show. My many patrons had agreed to give it their support and it promised to be a success. But on the great day not a soul turned up. The hotel was full of people, bustling around excitedly and drinking in the bar. This was the day the Japanese bombed Pearl Harbour, 7 December 1941. Everyone was so absorbed with the news, they had no time for so frivolous a thing as an exhibition of pictures.

Nyali

Our rented bungalow at Nyali on the Mombasa mainland across a pontoon bridge from the island, was one of about half-a-dozen such bungalows built chiefly for the holiday traffic. The bungalows were made of coral blocks thatched with palm leaves, and the walls were clear of the roof to allow the air to circulate and keep the rooms as cool as possible. The situation of these bungalows was enchanting. They were surrounded by coconut palm trees and were within a hundred yards of the sea, across a beach of pure white sand.

As you walked along the beach you saw it was covered with little round holes: the homes of innumerable crabs. As one approached they dived *en masse* into their holes with their little bright eyes shining if you looked closely. Johnny, our brindle bull terrier, made many attempts to catch them, but they were too quick for him. Later when the troops arrived and bathed from the beach, the crabs disappeared.

Outside in the sea, about half-a-mile from the shore, is a coral reef protecting the inner waters against the heavy seas, and what was important for the bathers, keeping out the sharks. It was possible to walk and wade out to the reef at low tide, with short swims in the deeper water. Children used to walk in it barefoot, but I had seen little yellow spotted snakes, so I wore sand shoes. At high tide we had anchored a small raft in the water about 50 yards out.

Owing to the rationing of petrol, our movements at Mombasa were very restricted. A trip into town and back, to buy our groceries once a week was the extent of the use of our car. My wife, however, resourcefully suggested a solution. That was to apply for a special permit in order to hold an exhibition of pictures at Malindi, a distance of some 30 miles up the coast to the north-east, and a permit was granted on that condition.

Malindi

We booked rooms at Lawford's Hotel, owned and run by an old friend, Commander Lawford. My experience with the recent exhibition at the Manor Hotel in Mombasa was fresh in my memory, and I would have avoided the show if I could. But every morning at breakfast my host would enquire in a loud voice, 'When are we going to have this exhibition of paintings of yours, Nestor?' It was in fact a fine advertisement for me. The interest of the guests was aroused and stimulated by the repetition of the remark. Consequently when I held my exhibition, I sold all my pictures and we not only paid for our holiday but returned home with funds.

There were a number of good hotels in Malindi. It was a gay little holiday resort, with plenty to see in the neighbourhood. The bathing is good but can be dangerous owing to the currents; while we were there the sea water was a bright orange due to the erosion. The mouth of a small river was about a mile up the coast and the recent heavy rains must have brought large quantities of soil from along its course.

Vasco da Gama landed at Malindi in 1498, and there is a tower erected on a headland to his memory. Here also were a number of phallic pillars of which

The ruins of Gedi

Beach scene at Nyali

very little is known. They are situated near a charming but delapidated bazaar with a courtyard, in the middle of which a huge flamboyant tree was growing. We stopped the car to admire the profusion of vermilion flowers with which it was covered and the long seed pods which cast their shadows on the whitewashed walls of an adjoining house. As we watched a number of children trooped down an open staircase. They were Indians and Swahilis, dressed in a variety of coloured costumes as they emerged from school to make a picture for me which I quickly sketched.

Within a few miles of the hotel there were two sights well worth seeing. The first of these was known as the 'Blue Lagoon' and it deserved its name. The little bay is surrounded by coral outcrops fringed with coconut palm trees. The vivid blue sea with the complementary coloured yellow palm leaves combine to make a most brilliant scene. It was an ideal spot for any beachcomber to live, but very hot; so much so, that one of my lady passengers found when she got out of the car, that the back of her dress was stained red from the leather seat of the car.

Gedi

Not far from this was the second site we visited. This was the old ruined town of Gedi. Nothing is known about it, nor of the circumstances which caused it to be abandoned. It is quite a mystery. When we first saw it, the ruined town

Malindi,
children on a staircase

which extended over many acres was buried in dense forest. You would see an arched gateway leading into a courtyard from which a baobab tree would be growing, or there was what appeared to be a swimming pool, the walls covered with creepers and the stem of a Casuarina tree which had forced its way through the broken cement. It was difficult to penetrate far owing to the dense tree growth. These trees, many of them over 30 feet high, must have taken many years, perhaps centuries to grow. The whole place was worthy of being preserved exactly as it was. It was unique. But this was not to be. The next time we saw it some years later, the trees had been cleared, the walls nicely cleaned and the paths made for our convenience. There was a turnstile and a ticket office where you contributed your sixpence to pay for all this 'improvement'.

We enjoyed the first year of our residence in Mombasa, but the conditions were unsuitable for a long stay, and when our two-year contract to rent our bungalow was up, we decided to leave. The difficulty was to find a house in Nairobi; but fortunately for us we learnt that a very good house was available in six month's time on the farm adjoining our own at Kipkarren, in the meantime we rented a house a Moiben near the Sergoit Rock.

So we packed our belongings into our Dodge car and set off on our travels. The two years in an open garage at the coast had not improved it, nevertheless I was offered twice as much for it as I had paid five years earlier; but I could not accept as I would not have been given a permit to buy a new car.

The road from Mombasa to Nairobi was interesting but the surface was rough, and it was very lonely. The total distance is 350 miles and for stretches of 50 or 100 miles there was no habitation. As the war was on, petrol was rationed, so we met no cars or other traffic.

Every now and then we stopped to admire the view and I made sketches. We saw on our journey the famous Ngorongoro Crater, about 35 miles in circumference which teems with game of every description: here are lion, leopard, eland, kongoni hartebeest, as well as buck and many kinds of gazelle, all easily viewed safely from the rim of the steep walls of the crater. Some people have even seen lions stalk their victims in broad daylight and make a kill; but even without such an excitement the experience is considered to be the finest of its kind available to the lover of wild life. But it is difficult to reach without a guide and a powerful car as the road winds through dense forest and the climb to the lip is very steep.

Moiben

The farmhouse we rented at Moiben was built of wood. It was situated at the top of an escarpement with a fine view down to a river and a range of hills across a broad plain.

This was another house which had been left untenanted for over a year, but instead of snakes and rats, this time we found it infested with fleas. Every room had them, and we spent the first few days washing the floors with paraffin. It was a farm of over a thousand acres, and while we were there we were visited regularly by a herd of about 20 giraffe. They apparently roamed about throughout the district as we saw them while out for a drive some ten miles away. It is curious that they are not afraid of a car and will allow it to approach to within a few yards, but they keep their distance from any human being on foot.

The squatters left on this farm were Masai, and they had a large herd of cows. I warned them they were not allowed to burn the grass for grazing. But they took no notice and one day they started a fire to windward of the house, which was a serious threat to it. Every available person was collected to beat it out, and I directed operations. Suddenly the wind changed towards me. The smoke was so dense I found I could not breathe and wondered if I could last much longer. But I was rescued by a Kikuyu garden boy who lead me to a roadway, which was a natural firebreak, otherwise I might have been burnt to death. Curiously enough, we read in the paper of a farmer in similar circumstances, trying to put out a fire on his farm who had been trapped in the blaze and had died. The police to whom I reported our fire were very helpful. They impounded the cows belonging to the Masai squatter and he was heavily fined.

The great Rift Valley of which the Red Sea is a portion and which extends through Lake Rudolf in Kenya and past Lake Nyasa as far as Beira, also passes near this farm. The finest view of the Rift is from a scarp which can be reached by car up a steep road. This is the most magnificent view I have ever seen. As you peer over the edge you get the impression of looking into a vast limpid pale blue sea. The drop is some two thousand feet below and you see the flat surface of the valley, a faint yellow with blue patches of cloud shadows and little lakes. While we were watching an eagle dived down; it was the most spectacular dive it is possible to imagine as it became smaller and smaller and was lost to sight.

Eventually we reached our destination at Kipkarren. The house we rented was the best in the district. It was built in the Colonial Dutch style with a number of ornate gables. The main feature of the interior was a fine big room 30 feet long with a high arched ceiling supported by massive timbers, the walls were panelled in cedar and it was well furnished. There were ornaments which the owner had brought from Zanzibar, and a fine Lamu chest on which was placed a superb Russian icon. It was in fact surprising to find a residence of this standard in so remote a part. In addition there were three or four bedrooms and a tiled bathroom. There was also a cellar. The owner who had died some months previously had been a chemist, and one of his hobbies was to brew his own liquor. He made a mead from honey which we had often enjoyed when he was alive. As a perfectionist he decided to have it properly matured, so he poured the mead into a barrel, which he stored in the cellar, intending to allow it to ripen for a year. But when he tried to drain it off, there was none there. His servant had drunk the lot.

Return to Kipkarren

There was a crying need for greater production in Kenya owing to the war, which was one of the reasons for our decision to return to Kipkarren and develop a small virgin farm which we still possessed. We had expected to be welcomed back by our old acquaintances and neighbours in our district and we were somewhat surprised to find that they were all so busy they had hardly enough time to stop and say 'Good morning'. The slump was a touch of nature which made us all friends, but they were now prosperous. The prices of farm produce had risen considerably during the war. Whereas 'posho' had been

Our rented bungalow at Nyali, Mombasa, where we lived for two years

Coral outcrop at Nyali

Mombasa viewed from the mainland

5 shillings a bag before we left Kipkarren it was now 40 shillings. In addition government insured the farmers against loss by allowing them a grant of £2 per acre for ploughed and planted land. One farmer told me he had ploughed and planted 2,000 acres and was assured of £4,000 whatever the success or failure of the crop may be, he was 'sitting pretty'. Later governments sent inspectors and no payment was made unless the land was kept clean and properly farmed.

The farmers were prosperous. They had paid off their debts to the Land Bank and were working hard. They had had a long and difficult time during the slump, as we well knew, and we sympathised with them. But they didn't want competitors. That was not all. They had a scheme to enlarge the areas of their farms. And they recommended to government that land was to be compulsorily resumed, and my farm was included in their scheme. Their argument was, to the effect that no arable land should be left vacant, which could be employed to grow crops badly needed to help the war effort for production. It was a very laudable notion, but unfair to those who had joined the forces or had been away on active service with the troops.

The Nandi Native Tribe

Nandi

My farm at Kipkarren was situated at the apex of a salient of small 160-acre farms protruding into the Nandi Native Reserve. This salient was included in the Soldier Settlement Scheme, as it was excellent well-watered soil suitable for the cultivation of coffee.

But the loss of this area was by no means acceptable to the natives who continued to consider it their property. And government subscribed to the justice of their claims by allocating the rents, paid by the farmers, to Nandi funds. Nevertheless the impression remained that it was not altogether satisfactory, and our provincial commissioner, when he heard that I intended to build on our farm, strongly advised against my doing so, since it was in such an isolated position.

The Nandi are a proud warlike people and the British Administration had a long history of opposition from them dating back to 1895, when the first Nandi outbreak occurred.

Two white traders who had penetrated into their country were murdered, and punitive measures were taken against them which were largely inconclusive. The tribe continued their opposition by interfering with the construction of the Uganda Railway, stealing the iron rails and fittings, so that further punitive measures were taken in 1900 and 1903.

Another cause of trouble with the Nandi was their refusal to pay their hut tax, and matters came to a head as a result of an unfortunate incident, when a Nandi was shot by an askari. As a reprisal nine askaris were killed, and the commissioner sent a native clerk to the Nandi chief demanding the immediate payment of the outstanding hut tax. The chief replied by returning the clerk's head, with the message: 'This is the hut tax of the Nandi'.

It was then decided that the situation required exceptional measures, and a strong force of King's African Rifles was sent, which captured large numbers of cattle, sheep and goats.

A well-known libon, or witch-doctor, was recognised as being at the root of all the trouble, and a KAR officer was sent to discuss peace terms with him. The libon arrived with his followers, and held out his hand holding tufts of grass as a symbol of peace. As he did so, one of his followers fired an arrow which struck the helmet of an officer, who immediately retaliated by firing his revolver killing the libon. This put an end to further trouble from the tribe.

This was past history and I found the Nandi a most reasonable people, with a variety of interesting manners and customs.

The tribe consists of as many as 17 clans each with its respective totems including most of the animals, birds and insects with which they are familiar such as the lion, elephant, hyena, colobus monkey, duiker and snake, also the crested crane, buzzard and partridge as well as the chameleon, soldier-ant and bee.

Of these the animal held under the most respect and fear is the hyena, which has been aptly described as the living mausoleum of their dead. An imitation of the cry of the hyena may be punished with the penalty of death or refusal of a husband or wife in marriage.

The Nandi have a remarkable control over the totems attached to their respective clans, as related by A.C. Hollis, a former administrative officer in Kenya, in his book *The Nandi, Their Language and Folk-Lore* in which he mentions a personal experience of the control exercised by the Nandi over their totem. He relates how he pitched his camp at the foot of the Nandi escarpment, when a swarm of bees attacked his safari and all their efforts to destroy them were useless, until a Nandi volunteered to quiet the bees.

'He was practically stark naked, but he started off at once to the spot where the loads were, whistling loudly, in much the same way as the Nandi whistle to their cattle. We saw the bees swarm round him, but beyond brushing them lightly from his arms he took no notice of them, and still whistling loudly proceeded to the tree in which was their hive. In a few minutes he returned, none the worse for his venture, and we were able to fetch our loads.'

The Nandi are experienced apiarists and frequently brought their honey for me to buy. They tie hollow tree trunks into the branches of trees to encourage the swarms to settle there, but they had a bad habit of cutting down a tree if a hive happened to be inaccessible.

One morning, a couple of Nandi turned up with a quantity of excellent honey, which they sold to me with many expressions of pleasure and amusement.

Later, while walking round some forest on my farm, I discovered a fine old tree near the Nandi Border cut down merely to get a few pounds of honey in the trunk. The police and two Nandi detectives soon discovered the culprit. It was my herd boy who admitted he had cut down the tree. So he was taken to Eldoret and sentenced to a short term of imprisonment. We were in Eldoret shopping, when I heard a greeting of 'Bwana, Bwana,' and there was the herd boy all smiles, he had finished his punishment and would like a lift home. So he jumped into the back of my car like an old friend, without any sign of resentment and resumed his old job.

The staple food of the Nandi, like those of all the other tribes in Kenya, is posho or mealy-meal, made from Indian corn, which they grow in patches around their huts. And they also cultivate such vegetables as they are able, but they may be seen plucking leaves and collecting herbs growing among the rough grass on the farm, and when asked what it was, they said 'mboga' – vegetables; there was certainly plenty of wild mustard about, which they may have used as seasoning.

Nandi elmoran

One one occasion, while driving my car accompanied by a servant, at the start of the rainy season, we saw a native seated on an outcrop of rock diligently beating a tattoo with a stick on one of the rocks. On my return some time later he was there beating his tattoo. My servant explained that he was encouraging a swarm of termites to emerge from their nest by imitating a heavy downpour of rain and this had the desired effect. Millions of flying ants emerge from their holes in a solid column which continues for ten minutes or longer, and they can then be packed in gunny bags to be carried away for food. The ants soon shed their wings and they are considered to be delicious; early explorers have testified to that.

Recently, it has been stated that there are schemes to cultivate termites for their nutritional value and for profit. Experiments have proved that the protein extracted from termites is very high, and the oil extract would also be very profitable.

Nandi girl

Nandi girl

Initiation Ceremonies

In addition to the 17 clans of the Nandi, there is another sub-division resulting from the circumcision ceremony, which takes place every seven-and-a-half years and establishes an 'age group' of young men who form a close association to help and support each other.

The circumcision or initiation ceremony is a very important and indeed essential part of the tribe's social structure. It is the ceremony marking the transition both for girls and boys from the state of childhood into a new stage of life.

The boys go off in small bands into the forests and live as best they can by their own efforts. This scheme is devised to teach them resourcefulness and courage. They were quite willing to be sketched. Their arms, legs and faces were painted with white clay and they carried bows and arrows and a knob kerry or arrow 'to aim at girls who came to peep'. But the most remarkable part of the costume was a grass head-dress, without which they were not supposed to be seen. This head-dress, made of long grass like a cone, extended from just above the knees to a topknot high above the head. Two holes were made in the grass opposite the eyes and bound with twine to allow them to see, but otherwise there was very little ventilation. A number of dead mouse birds were left dangling from this head-dress which was erected up to seven feet high.

The girls also had their distinctive costume, and they were not supposed to be seen by men, but the prohibition did not apply to me. They were quite pleased to allow me to sketch them.

Their costumes consisted of the regular long leather garment reaching from just below the shoulders down to the ankles, and bound at the waist with a belt. Their bare arms and feet were coloured with red or yellow ochre, and they wore the customary coiled wire ornaments on legs and arms and carried a stick.

Like the boys, they should not expose their heads and therefore wore a leather head-dress with two holes to see through. Their hair was dressed into thin ringlets plastered with ochre and their ears, which were generally in the process of having the lobes elongated, were plugged with circular pieces of wood or even an old jam tin two or three inches in diameter. This must have been very painful and liable to infection, judging by the appearance of some which looked as though they were festering. But they bore it with fortitude. Their curious head-dresses which made them look like diminutive members of the Ku-Klux-Klan, were a source of danger to them as they could not see where they were walking. At times we encountered them in the main road while driving the car, and they blundered about without knowing where they were running.

In the rain their leather garment made a most efficient umbrella. One day, as we were returning from the post, it came on to rain heavily; pouring down in sheets, so much so that I decided to stop the car as I approached a dangerous slippery drift over a culvert on a curve. While waiting we saw two curious figures approaching up the hill. As they got nearer we saw that they were two young girls, gaily splashing along through the slush. They had their skirts inverted to cover their heads, naked from the waist downwards.

The hairstyles for the women have significance; for example, if it should be twisted into thin strings and plastered with ochre, it means that she is pregnant.

Nandi boy and girl before circumcision ceremony

It is intended as a safeguard for her. Normally the heads of all men, women and children are shaved frequently and this would be necessary from the point of view of cleanliness, since the hair is so frequently plastered with mud.

Nandi Costume

The older men and women or 'wazee' are interesting and very dignified. A 'baraza', or council, of old men seated together, every now and then taking a pinch of snuff, reminds one of a collection of old roués. One old man whom I used as a model, called at our house regularly to ask me to give him permission to graze his oxen on some crown land, known as the Sorora Hills. It was useless for me to protest that it was not in my power to do so, as the land did not belong to me. He was a striking-looking figure with a feather stuck in the mat of his greying hair. Many years later, I did an oil painting from a sketch of him which was sold and taken to America.

The older men also wear a single garment made of goat skins, which is suspended from one shoulder and doubled across the body, covering the left arm completely but leaving the right arm free to hold a stick which they invariably carry. The upper part of the ear is pierced with a small hole. This is a tribal mark similar to that of the Masai. The lower part of the ear or lobe is divided in childhood to hang down for about three inches and carries an ornament at the end. They also wear coiled wire on their arms, and necklaces of cowries or straps. It is practically a uniform for the older men.

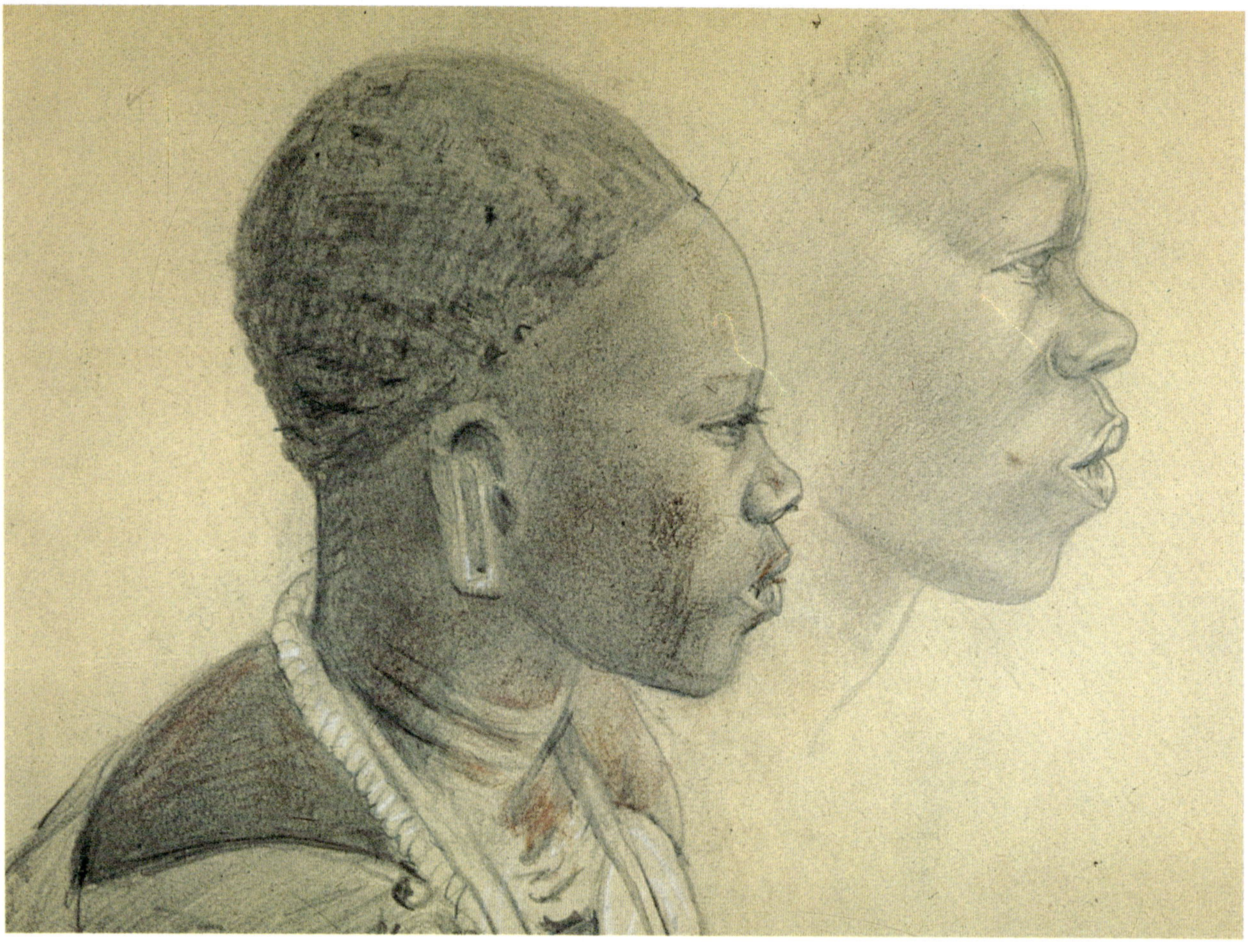

Nandi girl

The young men, elmoran or warriors, seem to have discarded this uniform of their elders, and generally wear a pair of shorts and a sheet or shawl of 'American' cloth dyed yellow or red, tied at the waist. They are, however, very particular about their head-dress, which is elaborately curled and plastered with ochre to form a pigtail, which is supported in a holder. They also wear the necklaces, bangles and ear ornaments.

One very striking and decorative feature of the Nandi costume is the overall garment, made of a patchwork of goat skins. These skins are cured and smooth on the inside, but the squares and oblong shapes on the outside are left in their natural state. They present quite a barbaric effect with the odd shapes of the hair markings, black and white or red, of which the goat skins are composed.

The supply of so many decorative models to draw from inspired me to start work again with enthusiasm. Fortunately, they were quite willing to accept this type of employment, not so much for the money, as for the new interest it gave them.

This attitude was very different from that of the Swahilis in Nairobi, who were probably prostitutes and considered they were underpaid at 3 shillings an hour, although at that time a model in London was not paid more than 5 shillings an hour. But their reluctance to stand as models may have been because they were Mohammedans, and their religion forbade the representation of the human figure. The Kikuyu were far more attractive that the Swahili with their head-dress of bunches of coiled wire or mauve-coloured material.

Nandi Elmoran, a young warrior

So I engaged three Nandi models, an old man, a young man or moran and a woman. They took a great interest in the sketches, and were very outspoken critics; praised any work of which they approved, but did not hesitate to condemn a failure.

Unlike many other natives who apparently could not understand a picture and would hold it upside down, the Nandi were genuinely interested. When we first arrived, we were clearing out a lot of old newspapers and other junk left by a previous occupant of the house, among which were some illustrated papers. One of our helpers picked up a picture and went off into fits of laughter, which was echoed by his companions. I was curious and went to see what it was all about. But I was surprised to find that the amusement was over a very ordinary photograph of a royal lady in full regalia, decked out with a crown and masses of pearl and diamond necklaces. To my mind there was nothing funny about it.

The first day my models came to work, I explained to them what I required – that they should be at ease and stand still. The young moran was a fine strong-looking fellow, but he stood for little over five minutes when I saw him sway and tumble over onto his back. At first I thought it was put on in order that he should not be made to pose too long, but I could see from his face and head which was covered in sweat, that it was a genuine faint. It never occurred to me that they could be affected by the heat or the sun as they are always out in it without any head protection. I thought perhaps he might be trying to hold his breath, but probably it was because he was not moving about. However, I hastened to explain to him that the sun's rays were very strong, otherwise I might have been accused of having the evil eye.

After this, all of them were very good models and could resume a pose very accurately after a short rest.

They were also satisfied that they were receiving preferential treatment in comparison with the ordinary farm labourer to whom I paid the same wages.

It was here that I learnt that my retrenchment had been a blessing in disguise, as this outdoor sketching practically restored me to normal health once more.

Building our House and Life on the Farm

I had made up my mind to build a small house on our farm, which was within easy walking distance of the house we had rented in Kipkarren.

The war was still on, and building materials and tools were not only in short supply but practically unprocurable without a permit. However, I was fortunate in meeting a friend who had a large collection of tools beyond his requirements, and he very kindly allowed me to buy them. Providentially, also, a farmer who was leaving the district had burnt bricks for sale. They were of poor quality, and I had to buy 50 per cent more than I needed, as they broke each time they were loaded onto and unloaded from the lorry; but I had no suitable clay on my own farm for brickmaking so this supply was invaluable.

We also had no trouble with labour. The Nandi were very interested in the building. It was new to them and a relief from the tedium of tribal life, or employment as farm labourers picking coffee or cutting grass. Their wages were of little consequence to them, as there was nothing on which to spend the money, with no nearby shops. All they needed money for, was the payment of their hut tax, 12 shillings per hut collected by government once a year.

Our first problem was to clear and level the site of the house and lay out the foundations according to our plan. There was a certain amount of rock outcrop on the farm, and I decided to make the foundations of broken stones and rubble. This job of breaking stones was not popular and I had to be very tactful with them. Fortunately, they had a sense of humour as well as a tendency to avoid hard work. So, when I was approached to provide night watchmen to prevent these foundations from being broken, I replied, 'What, break up the stones? If they want to do that, send them along, I will pay them.' It was a poor joke, but luckily served its purpose.

Another time, I arrived at the building site early in the morning to put the men on their jobs, only to be told that they were not going to work any more. 'Very well,' I said, 'we will not build the house, and we will go to Nairobi'. Which we did for a month. On our return we were met with smiles of welcome and all were ready to work with a will.

An amusing occurrence happened one day when I had to go to Eldoret by myself and left my wife to supervise the labour. We were building the roof and panels of asbestos were being nailed between the joists. This was not strong material and failed to stand the weight of one of the natives, up above, who tried to walk across. He landed with a crash at my wife's feet and she got such a shock she nearly burst into tears thinking he had been killed; he, however, was not at all hurt and jumped up with a laugh. The incident was considered to be very amusing to the Nandi.

With the laying of the foundations, time for the difficult business of building the house had arrived, and by another fortuitous circumstance I was able to procure some of the very best assistance.

Italian POWs

There was a large Italian Prisoner of War camp at Eldoret, and those prisoners who wished to accept employment on farms were permitted to do so. They were given their rations and a fixed wage, and their employers provided quarters and transport, and generally augmented their food supplies and appointed a servant to cook and look after them.

Italians are recognised as being fine artisans and builders, and many farmers were glad to take the opportunity of employing them to build houses and dams. In spite of this, it was a toss-up whether one got a good worker or not. It had to be taken into account also that as there was a war on and they were enemies, they sometimes took reprisals by refusing to do a fair day's work, or even indulging in sabotage. As enemies also, they undermined the prestige of the British with the natives. The English were unable to speak Italian, but the Italians soon learned to speak Swahili, the *lingua franca* of Kenya, and conversations between the two were carried on in that language. This had the effect of classing the Italians with the natives, and they fraternised with them.

When we decided to build our house I applied to the POW camp for a carpenter and a mason. They worked very well, but, whether by accident or design, the spirit level was dropped and I had to return them for a week or longer till it was repaired.

The building progressed with frequent changes of workers from the camp, as they became slack or we found that they had little or no experience of the job

A forest in the Nandi reserve which was just behind our farm

they had to do. A serious setback occurred when I foolishly handed out our nails whenever they asked for them. As we began to build the roof, I suddenly discovered that all the large nails had disappeared; they had been exchanged with the natives for eggs or drink. I was unable to get a permit from the

The red road from Mombasa to Nairobi as it was when we travelled down it, during the rains it was impassable

Production Board to buy more large nails, and this held up building operations for over a month. Eventually, I was able to exchange a quantity of inch nails for some 'cut' nails kindly supplied by the railway. In this way, with delays, the building of the house took over a year to complete. But when it was finished, we were delighted with it. We had been lucky in finding two excellent masons who built arches between the rooms and a large bow window, which I would never have been able to undertake by myself. And one of them helped me, with the aid of instructions from a book called *Every Man His Own Builder* to lay a parquet floor, of which we were all very proud.

From this book I had already worked out the quantities of bricks required for the walls, and the dimensions of the timbers for the roof and ceilings.

It was while we were building our house that peace was signed, and the Italian Prisoners of War became collaborators instead. As a result, far more friendly relations were established, and many of them applied to remain on in Kenya as settlers.

At last we had a house of our own again. It did not leak, nor did the fireplace smoke. And our furniture and Persian rugs looked quite well on the polished floors, while my own pictures hung on the white distempered walls.

As yet we had no electric light, and our night time illumination was supplied by kerosene power Tilley lamps; and our water supply was limited to the capacity of a couple of two-thousand gallon corrugated-iron tanks in which the rain water off our corrugated-iron roof was stored. We would have liked tiles but even a permit for the minimum quantity of corrugated iron was given very grudgingly.

Dairy Farming

The next step was to erect a number of paddocks with posts and barbed wire for our small herd of cows. We were, of course, very dependent on them for our milk supply. I was surprised to learn how difficult it was to milk a cow. They were very temperamental and would only allow themselves to be milked by the milkboy. One morning when he was ill, I told one of the other servants to do the milking. And when he protested that he couldn't do it, I thought, what nonsense, I will do it myself. The cow was in the shed tied up and ready. I was aware that it is necessary to encourage it to give its milk by permitting the calf to start the flow. When this had begun I took over, but the cow immediately dried up. It turned round and gave me quite a quizzical look, as much as to say, 'Stop your tickling, Jock'.

Even the Nandi, expert cattle thieves as some were, were baffled by our cows which 'escaped' one night. I had built them a lock-up shed made of wattle poles with a thatched roof, which they greatly appreciated. It was amusing to see them troop down to the shed when it started to rain. We considered that this protection, which of course could only be provided for very small herds such as ours, about a dozen in all, was responsible for the very low mortality among the calves, which is generally the highest cause of loss in a herd. However, the night our small herd 'escaped' was when I had instructed one of the boys to lock the shed. We were awakened after midnight by the pounding of hooves around the house, and there were all our cows obviously determined not to be driven away from a comfortable home.

We got to be very fond of those cows and discovered that they had many human qualities and failings. One little bull was very inquisitive, particularly when we had visitors. He would walk up to the house and peer in at the windows, indeed he even made an effort to enter an open door. But what we found most interesting was to watch the miracle of a calf being born. It was amazing to see how quickly the little animal burst as it were into blossom. Within a few minutes, perhaps a quarter of an hour, it would struggle to its feet and totter about and within a very short period it would be kicking up its heels and jumping for joy.

We left our first little calf in charge of the house boys while we went for a walk round our lake and on our return went up to see how it was getting on. There was no sign of it. But we discovered the boys working away at a hole in the ground. And there was our calf just visible down a deep ant-bear hole. It was extracted with difficulty but appeared to be none the worse for its first adventure in its new life.

This little calf we called Snowdrop, she was pure white and the idol of our small herd, particularly of our little bull while it was still young, and, in fact, afraid of the big cows. But he loved Snowdrop and it was touching to find how grateful he was to me, when Snowdrop was indisposed and I made her well by giving her a dose of liquid paraffin which fortunately did the trick. He was a very pretty little bull with a face like a pansy and as he grew up developed into a fine animal. Unfortunately, we were persuaded by some neighbours to exchange him for one of their bulls on the grounds that we required a change of new blood, as he was born of our own cows on the farm. We had not definitely decided on the exchange, when one afternoon our neighbour sent their bull to our farm, accompanied by his cows, with a herd, and we foolishly allowed our bull to be returned in its stead. It was the last we saw of him. And we bitterly regretted the transaction as the bull we had received in exchange died of 'black quarter', within a week, and it might have affected the whole of our little herd. It is probable that we were entitled to demand the return of our bull but we decided not to act on this. But we considered it was a dirty trick by our neighbour.

One of the difficulties with regard to farming cattle is the ticks they get covered with. They need to be handpicked or driven through a cattle dip filled with disinfectant. Both processes to which they are very much averse.

Nandi Customs

The Nandi were insistent on what they considered to be 'man's work'. They would rarely work as house boys or cooks, but would act as cattle herdsmen or farm labourers. We had the greatest difficulty in persuading them to cut and bring our firewood from the forest, or carry the water to the house from our stream; two absolutely necessary jobs if we were to live on the farm at all. The women did not work for Europeans except as children's nurses. I had, therefore, to make a stand about the work we required.

The first man that refused to cut and bring the firewood was told that I would sign him off. After a while he returned and said he would agree to do so provided Kipkirkir, a rival of his, did it the following day. Once it was agreed to, they all carried on happily doing the 'footies' as it was called, a task which meant only a couple of hours' work per day.

An amusing example of 'man's work' was when a hefty policeman, who was sent as a guard for our house while we were away on a holiday, left his belongings in the hut he had been sleeping in. When I drew his attention to this, he replied. 'I can't carry that, I'll send my mother to bring it away.'

It was advisable to respect customs and prejudices. A farmer who insulted one of his labourers by calling him a '*nusu mtu*' or half-man, was attacked and killed by him. The murderer ran away and was sheltered by his friends, whom we learnt later, lived near our farm. The first we heard of the crime was from some of our own people, who asked us if the government would send a punitive force against the tribe. We explained that the only one who would be caught and punished was the murderer. But he was never given up by his friends, and escaped the penalties of the law as he committed suicide by hanging himself.

We engaged one curious character, not a Nandi, as a herd boy. He had a religious complex of some sort, as we would find him kneeling on the ground on the path in front of us when we were out for a walk. It was an attitude which invited an appropriate response but I thought it better to discharge him for inattention to his duties.

Generally we found the Nandi very reasonable and understanding. They accepted the fact that our farm was our property although they considered, as I have said, that the land rightly belonged to them. Eventually after we left, but before the country was handed back to the natives of Kenya, we learnt that the government had taken over all the farms in the Kipkarren valley – including our farm – which had been allocated to Europeans, and the whole area was bought by the Nandi.

Buffalo on the plains at Nairobi

There was a spring in the indigenous forest on our farm which we learnt, had been used from time immemorial in marriage and circumcision ceremonies. Consequently I was asked, when three Nandi girls were to be married, if they could use the spring for the nuptial bath customary before the marriage ceremony; which, of course, was agreed to.

One of the girls to be married was a relative of our gardener, and through him we received an invitation to the wedding. It was, unexpectedly, a very impressive ceremony. My wife, Dorothy, witnessed the bathing in the spring and the procession that followed when the attendants of the girls fanned them with palm leaves. In the meantime I waited on the hill above, and I was very surprised at the beauty and solemnity of the singing which accompanied the

Hippo at Mzima Springs

A typical Nandi hut

bathing. It reminded me of the services in one of our own cathedrals.

The brides were then taken away while a dance was performed by a number of young married women. No men were allowed to attend. However, I was permitted to watch from a distance. The dance, which was accompanied by singing, consisted of rhythmic movements, bending and flexing the legs while the time was marked by slapping the thighs in unison. The women were lined up in single file one behind the other under the control of a mistress of ceremonies.

After this, we congregated at the top of the hill and watched the arrival of the marriage cortège as it wound its way up towards us, led by our gardener with a dignified solo dance. The three brides were conspicuous in their brilliant red skin costumes as they halted on a little hillock surrounded by their male attendants with their spears flashing in the sunlight.

This was clearly a very important wedding as it was attended by some hundreds of Nandi from the district around and the Reserve.

We did not remain to see the completion of the ceremony which was long drawn out; but we understood that it terminated with a prolonged beer drink extending indefinitely till the supply of liquor, which had been stored for the occasion, was finished.

My gardener was indisposed after the event for at least three weeks, and he sent his wife to ask me to bring some medicine. He was a tall, elegant, rather delicate man, some years older than his pretty, very young, wife, who could do no wrong in his eyes. Every now and then he would come to ask for a few days off from work, as his wife had 'run away'. Whether it was an excuse for a holiday or a genuine occurrence, I never discovered.

The young girls from the Reserve were very provocative, they made a point of taking a short cut and walking past our servants' quarters although they were told not to do so. Our house servants were of a different tribe. One of these girls accused the cook of bewitching her so that she could not bear children. A party of her boyfriends came and complained to me and they were obviously out to make trouble. So we took the girl to be examined by a lady doctor on a nearby farm who pronounced her to be quite normal. The decision was accepted but it did not end the feud. A few nights later there was a loud knocking at our window and our servants told us that their huts had been set alight. They managed to escape with their belongings but the huts were destroyed. It was obvious that the Nandi were to blame but we could not prove that they were responsible, and we were put to a great deal of inconvenience till new quarters could be provided. This attitude of the Nandi towards our house servants made it very difficult for us to engage and retain them, and we spent many a fruitless day in Eldoret searching for new recruits.

This was a serious drawback to our residence on the farm, nevertheless we realised that we had to make an effort to be on friendly terms with the Nandi, on whom we were not only dependent for our farm labour, but who could have made it unpleasant for us. I therefore dispensed medicines as best I could. Every morning there was a sick parade. Usually children who responded readily to a dose of salts or who required their sore eyes washed with boracic. I got quite a reputation as a doctor and they preferred to come to me rather than be treated at a government dispensary some two miles away. Early one morning I was actually begged by some Indians to come and deliver the wife of one of them, who was on the point of having her baby. Needless to say, this was beyond my powers. But there were some serious cases which I had to take to the Native Civil Hospital in Eldoret; one of these was a boy who had a very swollen stomach, I was informed that he had been operated on but he had not survived. Another sad case was that of a baby girl, about a year old; she was the daughter of one of my models, and I was horrified to see that she had burnt the top of her head, presumably in the fire on the floor of the hut where she was put to sleep. It seemed incredible that her cries were disregarded. I took her to see a doctor but he advised that it was best left alone and kept clean. There was a danger that the shock would bring on pneumonia so Dorothy wrapped her in an old jumper, and it was pathetic to see how delighted the little creature was to acquire this bit of unexpected finery. We never saw the end of this as it occurred just before we left the farm, nor did we know what happened to my Nandi herd boy. One's servants in Kenya were always referred to as boys although they may have been men. He arrived one morning with the tips of the fingers of one hand literally eaten to the bone, and explained that it had been done by his brother the night before. It seemed beyond belief that he should have permitted the attack to reach so advanced a stage even if they had both been very drunk.

The Dam

My 160 acre A-farm at Kipkarren was badly supplied with water. There was a swamp in the middle between two hills, with a narrow outlet which suggested a possibility of conservation of the rainfall from the catchment area on the two sides. The Government Soil Conservation Service, under Colin Maher, advertised an offer to construct dams on farms where suitable. I applied and my application for a dam to be built was accepted.

Maher with his conservation team and two large bulldozers arrived, and completed the job with incredible speed in just three days. The dam was 450 feet long and cost about £50. First the bulldozers levelled the site, then they excavated soil at each end, and worked backwards and forwards evenly depositing the earth and levelling it at the same time. The width of the dam at the base was over 30 feet, and it tapered upwards to 10 feet for the road on top. On one side of the dam a broad spillway was left, to allow the original stream to continue its course, and at the same time to provide a means of discharging excess water in the event of a heavy downpour of rain.

The rains broke almost immediately, and within a month, there was a stretch of pure water making a lake of four acres, 16 feet deep surrounded by indigenous forest in which colobus moneys could be seen jumping about.

I intended to put Talapia in the lake and sell the fresh fish in Eldoret where there was a ready market. And now that I had plenty of water I could put in a pump and irrigate the land and grow fruit. The water supply increased the value of my farm considerably. I was the envy of other farmers in the district, who all clamoured to have dams made for them. But mine had been the only application and Maher had his programme to complete. This did not prevent his being bitterly attacked.

As the water rose to the level of the spillway, all the trees whose stems were under water started to die, they lost their leaves and gradually became bleached like a fringe of ghost trees along the water's edge, and they then fell into the water. It was disappointing and we could have avoided it by making the lake shallower.
Another mistake was failing to clear the swamp of all its grass and reeds before the dam was built, because as the time passed, the clear surface of the water was broken by little islands of weeds.

We tried to correct these faults by bribing our labour to go into the water and remove whatever they could, but in the end we had to accept it and found it was an advantage. Large numbers of water birds arrived and made their nests on the islands. Crested cranes could be seen doing their nuptial dance, while dab chicks and moorhens darted about. There were also wild duck, herons and ibises. One could see them during their flights suddenly discovering the new mirror of water below, and they would circle around and land with a splash. On occasions we would be visited by such rare birds as knob-billed ducks.

In addition to the water birds, our lake appeared to attract a larger number of the regular species such as hornbills, honey birds, rollers and shrikes; and game birds such as guinea fowl, francolin and bustards.

But the bird we favoured above all others was the glossy starling, a beautiful brilliant metallic blue bird. We fed them with breadcrumbs, and flocks of 50 settled on our lawns with their young.

Nandi girl

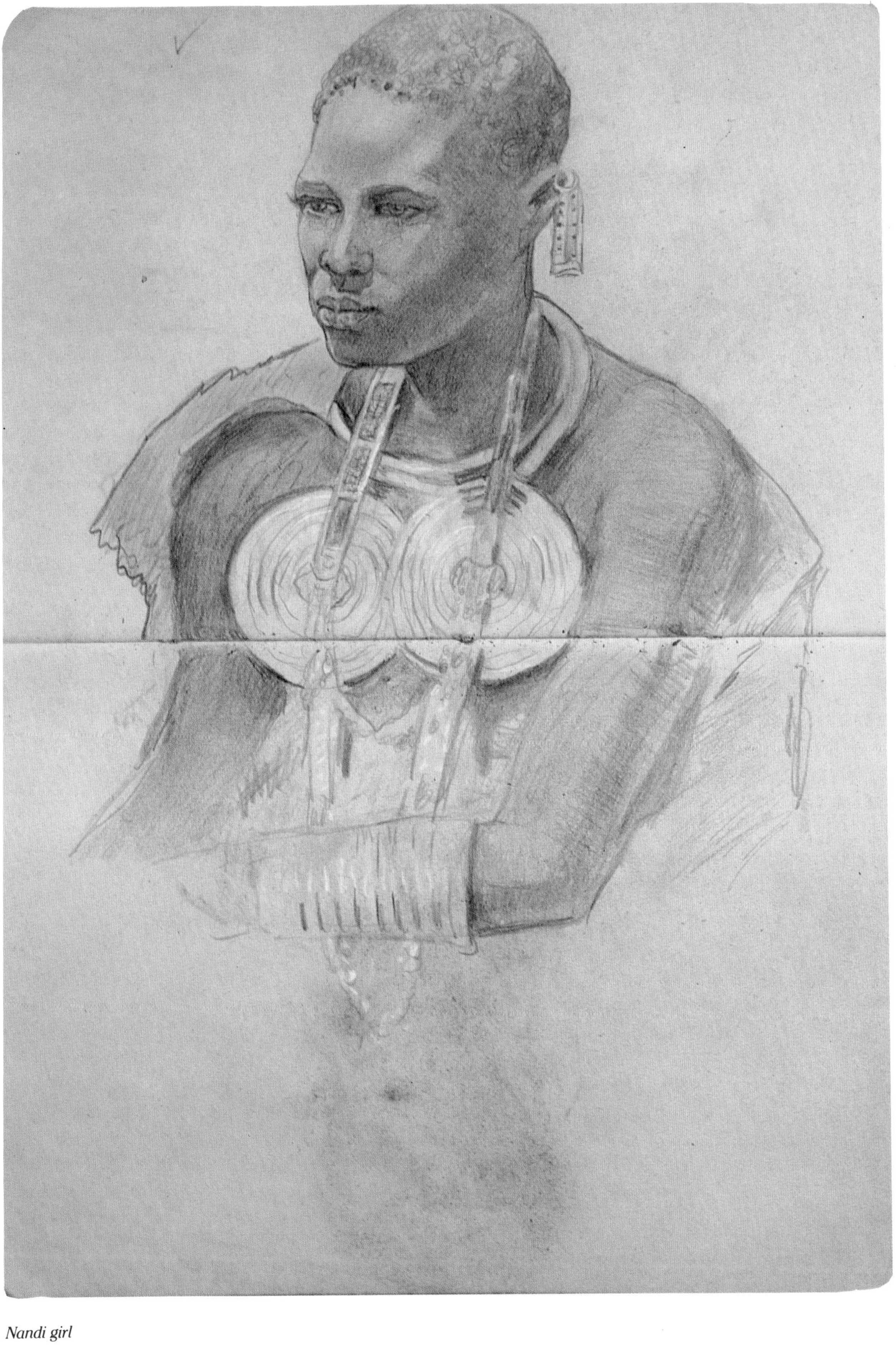

Nandi girl

Suk Tribesman in Ceremonial Headdress

Sale of the Farm

In 1947 the British evacuated from India and owing to the influx of new settlers from there, and also, as a result of the Soldier Settlement Scheme after the Second World War, there was a boom in land values.

An estate agent in Eldoret told me that there was a demand for small residential farms such as ours, and he advised me to take advantage of this and place the sale of our farm on his books. We were not anxious to sell but thought that, if the price was right, it might be of interest to see what demand there was.

The agent brought out prospective buyers, one of whom was a retired General who had travelled right across Africa from the West Coast, with his wife in their car without mishap. The lady was pleased with our farm and there appeared to be every prospect of a sale, but when they were about to leave it was discovered that, owing to our dreadful District Council roads, a spring in their car had been broken. And so the sale was off. We patched up the spring with a strong band of wire, but the damage was done.

In the meantime, we made enquiries about buying an alternative small farm, in the event of our selling; but we were astonished to find that all the properties we inspected were much more expensive than our own. They showed far less development and improvement. In one or two cases they did not even provide a house. So I immediately removed the sale of our farm from the books of the agent.

No sooner had this been done, than a Swiss doctor resident in Egypt, wrote to enquire if the farm was still for sale. I replied that it was not. However, he was so insistent that even when I explained our position and raised the price he immediately made an offer for it. It appeared that the isolation of the farm was an attraction to him, as well as the beauty of the situation with the lake and long views. So he quickly foreclosed on the deal and instructed the agents to affect a transfer. I had offered the farm for sale as it stood, including the cows and farm implements, as well as the furniture, my water colours on the walls and the Persian rugs we had bought at Christie's. All we retained was the car and our personal belongings.

This was in 1949 and within a few months of the sale, the pound was devalued by one-third. I wondered if perhaps he had inside information of the imminence of such a step. But I did not regret the sale.

Although we were sorry at the prospect of leaving our home, the sale had many compensations apart from the money. It repaid most of the losses I had sustained in previous farming ventures, and was somewhat in the nature of deferred savings. Also, the burning of the vegetation every year had become a nightmare; whenever we journeyed away from the farm and caught a view of it from a distance, there was invariably a spiral of smoke from a fire in the neighbourhood, and we dreaded finding on our return all our grassland and trees a black and charred mass. These anxieties were now a thing of the past and no longer our responsibilities. It was curious also, that while we were never

A married Nandi woman

Mountains of the Moon, on the borders of Uganda

afraid or nervous on the farm, surrounded as we were by primitive people, I noticed a feeling of relief when we left and lived for a time in the security of Muthaiga Club. I remembered how I had listened to every unaccountable sound in the stillness of the night. Our dog Johnny had died and I could not rely upon him any longer to give the alarm. Dorothy, on the other hand, missed her garden which she had taken such pains to make. It was not until she was in England that she felt, as she said, 'A lightness of heart, at dropping the white man's burden'.

And so while we planned how we would enjoy ourselves in London with its galleries and museums, we agreed to remain on at the farm for a month and savour the pleasures of an existence we would never experience again.

The Mountains of the Moon

We took advantage of the opportunity of spending a week at the 'Mountains of the Moon' and booked rooms at the Ruwenzori Hotel. On the way through Uganda we visited the main towns Jinja, Kampala and Entebbe. The Baganda women are attractively dressed in costumes which give the impression of European evening dress, they consist of highly-coloured materials, swathed around the body with a pannier effect, leaving the shoulders bare.

The last stage of the journey to Ruwenzori is along a narrow road with short runs and hairpin bends. One travels for mile after mile meeting very little traffic

Elephants on the route to Mombasa

Hippo, which were sometimes quite placid and approachable

till one becomes careless cutting corners, and an accident is avoided with only inches to spare.

The Mountains of the Moon is a long range of peaks which stretch across the horizon in front of the hotel, it has the reputation of being continually covered in clouds – which was as we saw it. Stanley, who discovered the range in 1875, was unaware of the snow-capped peak of Margherita, 16,815 feet high, as he camped on the Eastern slopes. There were interesting runs through lovely scenery to some Crater lakes, and many signposts along the road with the warning 'Beware of Elephants'.

On our return to Kipkarren we took a different route and stopped for the night at Tororo Rock. This is one of those curious geological formations, not uncommon in East Africa, consisting of an isolated rocky hillock, a hundred feet high or more, emerging abruptly from the surrounding level plain. At its base was a small private hotel which had gained quite a reputation on account of the eccentric behaviour of its owner. He was just as likely to refuse you accommodation if you should fail to please him on sight. We were unaware of that at the time, so we were somewhat surprised when on our enquiry if we might have a room and a bath to be told, 'If you don't have a bath it will be ten shillings extra.' This was said without a smile.

Last Days at the Farm

Now that we were about to leave our farm for good, we began to realise how much we would miss. It would chiefly be the contact with nature in a form such as we were never likely to experience again. This was probably one of the last places in the world unspoilt by civilisation.

I would miss my indigenous forest with the closely packed trees of many species – some not yet identified, but others well known, such as the rubber plant which exuded a white milk from a leaf pressed between the fingers, the wild bananas, giant tree ferns, and liana creepers as well as the wild hollyhocks and gladioli, but above all the magnificent blooms of gloriosa lilies growing in such profusion even over my coffee bushes.

I was never attacked by any animal or bitten by any insect, although I walked for hours through the long grass as high as my head, or fought my way through dense undergrowth in the forest where it was probable no white man had ever penetrated before. There were monkeys in the trees and leopards and snakes about but they did not resent my presence. Indeed, the beautiful and rare colobus monkeys soon learnt to accept me without fear.

I was in the habit of sitting still for hours sketching on a wall of our dam close to the forest, when without hearing a sound I would sense that I was not alone and gradually became aware that the trees around were alive with colobus. Perhaps they had come out of sheer curiosity, or maybe they wanted to cross some open ground to another belt of forest.

They are exclusively arboreal and vulnerable on the ground, as they do not run like other monkeys, but proceed in little jumps, and could easily be caught or run down by a dog. These rare and beautiful little creatures are black and white, with long white bushy tails and capes. If a troop is seen against the setting or morning sun jumping from branch to branch, their white hair shines like a halo. And as they do not raid the maize shambas, they do no harm and are protected by law, but this does not protect them from the vandals who shoot them to make karosses or hide rugs.

With their very distinctive colouring one would expect that the colobus were very noticeable, but on the contrary it seems to hide them, particularly if they sit on an old dead tree that has white patches where the bark has worn off.

We were sorry to be leaving Kipkarren, which had an atmosphere different to any other I had ever experienced. In this modern world of noise and hurry, it was a haven of peace and quiet. If you listened you could hear the distant call of a guinea fowl or the raucous complaining cry of the hornbill. There was a limpid magic in the long views over the rolling hills and valleys for thirty or forty miles on one side, and on the other stood the mighty cliffs of Mount Elgon away on the Uganda Border. But the mornings were most impressive. They were like the first dawn of creation; as though the world had been washed in dew and was still dripping wet and hushed with an air of expectancy. Every now and then the colobus monkeys in the trees of our indigenous forest would break out into a chorus. It was so appropriate to these surroundings as were these most charming little creatures themselves.

In the evenings as I turned on the Tilley lamp in the sitting room, this was the signal for a party of buck to arrive and eat our Barberton daisies. They knew they were perfectly safe. And in the sky we would see the two crested cranes, absolutely on time, flying home, repeating their well-known cry 'Wardle Wardle'. There was practically no gloaming. The setting sun dived below the horizon and in a few minutes we would hear the croaking of the frogs, the cicada singing his interminable song, or the distant howl of a hyena which make the African night.

RAY NESTOR

Author's Acknowledgements

I would like to thank the following for their help in publishing this book.

I owe particular thanks to Phyllis MacSimon for typing my manuscript.

D.L. Waters for photographing my portraits which hang in Muthaiga Club, Nairobi.

Eric Hartley for his valuable assistance and advice.

Mark Hayes-Fisher for the care with which he photographed my pictures.

Victoria Huxley for her sensitive editing of my memoirs into the final text.

Grant Bradford for his help in selecting the pictures as well as designing the book and encouraging us with this project and
Harry Ricketts for offering to be the publisher.